KARL BLANCHET and BORIS MARTIN

editors

Many Reasons to Intervene

*French and British Approaches
to Humanitarian Action*

HURST & COMPANY, LONDON

First published in 2006 by Editions Le Cavalier Bleu
as *Critique de la raison humanitaire*
© Editions Le Cavalier Bleu, 2006
This revised and updated English translation first published in the United
Kingdom in 2011 by C. Hurst & Co. (Publishers) Ltd.,
41 Great Russell Street, London, WC1B 3PL
© Karl Blanchet, Boris Martin and the Contributors, 2011
All rights reserved.
Printed in India

The right of Karl Blanchet, Boris Martin and the Contributors
to be identified as the author of this publication is asserted
by them in accordance with the Copyright, Designs and
Patents Act, 1988.

A Cataloguing-in-Publication data record for this book
is available from the British Library.

ISBN: 978-1-84904-142-3

This book is printed using paper from registered sustainable
and managed sources.

www.hurstpub.co.uk

CONTENTS

v

CONTENTS

ABOUT THE EDITORS

Karl Blanchet is Lecturer at the London School of Hygiene and Tropical Medicine. He is Senior Research Fellow and formerly the Director of Humanitarian Programmes at the Overseas Development Institute in London'. He is also the former Director of Handicap International UK. He has led emergency actions and development programmes, principally in Eastern Europe and West and East Africa. Karl regularly contributes to Le Monde Diplomatique.

Boris Martin is Editor of the French journal 'Humanitaire', published by Médecins du Monde-France. He is also an independent publisher and author of several essays and accounts.

ABOUT THE CONTRIBUTORS

Rony Brauman is Associate Professor at the Paris Institut d'Études Politiques, director of the Humanitarian and Conflict Response Institute (University of Manchester) and director of research at the MSF Foundation. He was President of Médecins Sans Frontières from 1982 to 1994. He is the author of several books on humanitarian issues, including *Penser dans l'urgence* (2006) and *La Médecine humanitaire* (2010).

Christophe Courtin is a sociologist and philosopher. He is Project Manager for a programme of support for civil society in Cameroon financed by the European Union. For five years he was in charge of the Projects Department of the Comité Catholique Contre la Faim et pour le Développement (CCFD). He worked for several years in Africa (Rwanda, Benin, Niger, Côte d'Ivoire) for different French and international NGOs after having held decision-making posts in France in the human resources departments of several large industrial companies.

James Darcy is Senior Research Fellow and former head of the Humanitarian Policy Group at ODI. An international lawyer by background, he worked for ten years with Oxfam as programme co-ordinator in Central Africa, the Balkans, the Middle East, and South & East Asia. His current research at ODI includes work on fragile states, aid risks, humanitarian engagement and the security-development interface. He currently sits on the Board of Oxfam GB.

Hugh Goyder originally trained as an economist. He was a UN Volunteer in India and then joined Oxfam in 1976. He was a Country Director for Oxfam in India from 1979–82 and then in Ethiopia from

1982–6, where he led Oxfam's response to the famine of 1984. From 1992 he worked for Action Aid UK as an Africa regional manager and head of impact assessment. Since 1998 he has been an independent consultant, with a special interest in impact assessment and the evaluation of humanitarian activities.

François Grünewald is a trained agriculturalist, Director General of Groupe URD (Urgence—Réhabilitation—Dévelopement) and former Director of the post masters diploma in humanitarian management at the University Paris XII at Créteil. François Grünewald used to work with ICRC, UN agencies and NGOs. He has been involved in several key evaluation processes in the last ten years in Asia, Africa and Latin America and Middle East. In particular, he was the technical team leader of the Cluster evaluation in 2009 and the team leader of the inter-agency real time evaluation in Haiti after the 2010 earthquake.

Adeel Jafferi was the Press Officer for Islamic Relief.

Sami Makki is Senior Lecturer at Sciences Po Lille where he heads a Master's degree in International Relations. He also teaches International Security and Strategic studies in Paris (La Sorbonne). He is Doctor of political sociology from the École des Hautes Études en Sciences Sociales (EHESS) in Paris, where he has been a research coordinator in charge of the Transformation of War programme within the Centre for African Studies for the past four years. He is the author of numerous articles and a French book entitled *Militarisation de l'humanitaire, privatisation du militaire* published in 2004.

David Rieff is an American nonfiction writer and policy analyst. His books have focused on issues of immigration, international conflict, and humanitarianism. He has published numerous articles in *The New York Times*, *The Los Angeles Times*, *The Washington Post*, *The Wall Street Journal*, *Le Monde*, *El Pais*, *The New Republic*, *World Affairs*, *Harper's*, *The Atlantic Monthly*, *Foreign Affairs*, *The Nation*, and other publications.

Philippe Ryfman is Professor and Associate Researcher in the Department of Political Science and European Center for Sociology and Political Science (CESSP) at the Sorbonne University of Paris I—Panthéon-Sorbonne. He is also a lawyer and completed a Masters in 'International Co-operation, Humanitarian Action and the Politics of Development' at the same university. Amongst his most recent publications are: *Une* *histoire de l'humanitaire*, Paris: Editions La Découverte: Repères. 2008; *Les ONG* Paris: Editions La Découverte: Repères, second edition, 2009. He has also contributed to numerous collective works and wrote the column 'Civil Society' in *Le Monde Economie*, the weekly economic section of the French daily newspaper.

Dr. Hugo Slim is a Visiting Fellow at the Oxford Centre for Ethics, Law and Armed Conflict at the University of Oxford and a Director of CforC Group in London. His most recent book is *Killing Civilians: Method, Madness and Morality in War*, Hurst (2007), Columbia University Press (2008).

Egbert Sondorp was Medical Director with MSF Holland during which time he became increasingly involved in health work in crisis areas and post-conflict settings. Subsequently, as Director of HealthNet International, he specialised in post-conflict health development. Egbert Sondorp is currently Senior Lecturer in Public Health and Humanitarian Aid at the London School of Hygiene and Tropical Medicine.

PREFACE

Rony Brauman

The 'French doctors'—first and foremost Médecins Sans Frontières (MSF)—have created a style of humanitarian action that combines intervention in conflict situations with critical speech. The humanitarian practices we use today originated in the United States, Great Britain and Switzerland. France was the last to join the group of so-called 'founder democracies' in the humanitarian field. A closer look reveals that it was by drawing on already existing forms of action that MSF gradually developed its particular brand of intervention, which combines relief practices learnt from the Red Cross with efforts to mobilise public opinion, using strategies invented by Amnesty International.

To understand the importance given today to humanitarian aid (often improperly called emergency aid) compared to other forms of assistance, we must trace the major steps and changes that have marked its development since the 1960s. The 1960s and 1970s constitute the great era of development. At that time, aid was seen as an accelerating factor of progress. Against the backdrop of the Cold War, the challenge was to reduce the North–South divide by mobilising and transferring material resources and know-how. Actors such as the British NGO Oxfam and the World Bank adopted similar approaches, although operating on very different scales. Wells and dams were built, new agricultural techniques were introduced and the development of peasant cooperatives were encouraged: aid was designed to induce economic, social and technical progress, the active principle of which was productivity. Aid organisations almost ignored the wars, in particular the Vietnam War, and were mobilising so-called anti-imperialist forces world-wide. Their war (which was also mine at the time), although undoubtedly inspired by considerations of humanity and justice, had nothing humanitarian about it, no more so than the support given to anti-colonialist movements in southern Africa. With the notable exception of the International Committee of the Red Cross (ICRC), humanitarian organisations did not intervene in armed conflicts.

This period ended in the late 1970s, as development theories and practices failed and Communism began the last stage of its decline. The next period began in 1979–1980, with the ousting of the Pol Pot Regime in Cambodia and relief operations for Vietnamese boat people in the South China Sea. It would end with the fall of the Berlin Wall, the war in Afghanistan and the Ethiopian famine. One cannot but notice the degradation of their populations and the humanitarian mobilisation that followed as examples of the symptomatic failure of these communist regimes. During the 1980s, collective economic and social rights gave way to individual civil and political rights. The period was marked by the rapid growth of humanitarian NGOs, both in France and in Britain. MSF was consolidated and new relief NGOs were formed, such as Médecins du Monde (MDM), Action Contre la Faim (ACF) and Handicap International (HI). During this period of considerable expansion, the media gave increasing coverage to relief NGOs and the general public discovered humanitarian action as a form of private international Ethics. Intervention budgets increased considerably and projects multiplied rapidly.

The 1990s were characterised by new forms of interventionism by the United Nations in the form of 'military humanitarian' operations. We all remember the televised landing of American marines in the port of Mogadishu. The first objective of the United Nations, under its new Secretary-General, Boutros Boutros-Ghali, was to establish peace in countries at war, bringing in their wake NGOs, which were playing an increasingly important international role. In Liberia, Sierra Leone and Angola, NGOs were asked by the UN to strengthen peacemaking missions, triggering new debates among them. On the one hand, they considered themselves in solidarity with the system and the objectives of the United Nations, and therefore tended to support peace processes initiated by the UN. On the other hand, they realised that these peace operations often involved sacrificing civilian populations in the 'wrong' camp—the Revolutionary United Front (RUF) in Sierra Leone, for example, or Union for the Total Independence of Angola (UNITA). It was therefore not always possible to help in an impartial way (i.e. only on the basis of need). The question of the independence of humanitarian NGOs, particularly those working in war situations, became more acute. Meanwhile, the nature of conflict appeared to be changing, as territories fragmented and the number of war actors proliferated, making humanitarian missions more complex and more dangerous, as in the Congo, Sierra Leone and Somalia.

Finally, in the first decade of the twenty-first century and following the 9/11 attacks, a kind of radicalisation of phenomena seen in the 1990s can be observed. A new East–West divide has appeared, not, as in the Cold War, between Capitalism and Communism, but between the Islamic and the Western worlds. And even if one disagrees with this description, the fact that today's superpower and its allies impose this scheme on the rest of the world has to be taken into account. In the eyes of donors such as the US or Australia, humanitarian NGOs must from now on act loyally and take part in what they consider to be a global war on Terror, once again raising fundamental questions concerning the intellectual and financial independence of NGOs.

For the first time—and this is not the only merit of this book—French and British humanitarian professionals have decided to discuss common themes related to humanitarian action. Even if there are major differences between the French and British/American approaches, on closer inspection these tend to become less clear-cut. In any case, the real area of division—of confrontation even—does not lie in the nationality or origin of NGOs, but in their position in relation to the new geopolitical world order (mentioned above). In order to identify common ground, it is useful to understand the differences.

The first difference is a cultural one: we French tend to value controversy and debate, whereas our British colleagues tend to look for consensus. I have participated in numerous co-ordination meetings in the field where many nationalities were gathered around a table. The British are more at ease than the French with this type of exercise, no doubt because discussions take place in their own language, but mainly because they are used to institutional environments and co-management. In France, this type of relationship between NGOs and governments is beginning to develop, but is still limited. In my view, consultation with governments is not a desirable objective for NGOs operating in war zones. They should remain independent to the end, and it is difficult to see the advantage of consultation.

Another difference relates to the founding principles upon which an NGO is based. The main French NGOs were developed according to professions, 'professions without borders' so to speak. For example, MSF and MDM specialise in medicine, ACF in nutrition, and HI in physiotherapy and orthopaedics. British NGOs tend to be developed around themes, such as poverty (for Oxfam), children's rights (for Save the Children) and education (for Action Aid). The breadth or conversely the specialisation of the field of action has considerable influence on the way in which problems are posed and resolved. The third major difference relates to staffing. Although the French increasingly value their local teams, they tend to send large numbers of expatriates to the field, while British NGOs have preferred to recruit local staff. Finally, French NGOs are characteristically dispersed, in the image of France's 36,000 communes. That said, this dispersion is more apparent than real, as 80 per cent of financial resources are held by only a dozen NGOs.

One reason why some of the differences between French and British or American NGOs are diminishing is due to the development of international networks. In the case of MSF and its various national branches (Belgium, Netherlands, Spain, the United Kingdom and so on), we all work under the same banner, we adhere to the same Charter, we share the same objectives and our working language is more commonly English rather than French. However, MSF does have different ways of tackling problems. It is surprising to see how differently each branch interprets these principles of action. In this multicultural context, consensus is sought, but not at the cost of convictions! We have therefore had to learn to respect our different views, even when they lead to contradictions or inconsistencies within the group. MSF France is no longer the only voice of MSF. I imagine the same thing happened to Oxfam and Save the Children when they became internationalised.

There are a great number of NGOs, all of them publicising their actions and making their voices heard. These clash at times, but how could it be otherwise? These debates are not the sign of a 'humanitarian crisis', as some are too quick to point out; on the contrary, they are a sign of greater maturity. While changes have happened progressively and sometimes painfully, public support for humanitarian action has steadily increased. Nevertheless, the tsunami of December 2004 highlighted the limitations of the current debate, and the limited understanding among the public, the press—and quite a few NGOs—of relief in a natural disaster situation. It is dangerous to think that NGOs can reconstruct devastated regions, not only because they can't, but also because the backlash when they appear to fail is likely to be violent. It seems that France was the only country to have a confrontational—and often very lively—debate, pitting the French against each other and not against the British or Americans, on the question of the limitations of international aid. This debate is far from over and is not a national one. It concerns all aid actors. But this tragedy and the media coverage it attracted should not deter us from recognising the obvious: strengthened by years of experience drawn from British, American, Swiss and French sources, humanitarian action does not need to be constantly supported by the media in order to exist in the field. It has done so every day for a long time in countries where there is virtually no press coverage. This does not mean, however, that beyond the points of resemblance and difference, it should not take a critical look at itself.

1

THE BISHOP'S DIAGONAL VERSUS THE AXIS OF EVIL

STRATEGIES ON THE GEOPOLITICAL CHESSBOARD

Karl Blanchet and Boris Martin

The twenty years—'twenty glorious years'—between the Biafran conflict and the fall of the Berlin Wall saw non-governmental organisations acquire a very special place in the minds of citizens, and establish themselves as leading actors in international relations.

Nigeria, May 1968: the time when a new way of doing humanitarian action emerged. A year earlier, Biafra, part of one of the largest countries in Africa, had declared its independence. Determined to keep control of the province, rich in oil reserves, the Nigerian government surrounded it, causing a famine that hit eight million people. Despite news reports showing the horror of emaciated children, the UN was paralysed and states once again failed to give assistance to a suffering population in the name of national sovereignty and its corollary, non-interference in another state's internal affairs. France, busy managing its own May '68, was among them. Signing their contracts with the International Committee of the Red Cross (ICRC), men and women came to the rescue of 'the world's damned', only to break the pledge tying them to this 100-year-old institution, with its commitment to neutrality and discretion, when they saw the horror that was unfolding in Biafra.

1

In doing so, these doctors—among them Bernard Kouchner—were expressing an impulse which was to form the basis of a new form of humanitarian action: the need for testimony, for asserting the political dimension of medical action and for claiming the right to interfere: 'Who appointed us? No one; and that is what gives us our right. Human misery must never be a silent consequence of politics.' Kouchner often quoted Michel Foucault to explain this impulse of a few, an impulse which gave rise to the 'borderless' French movement called MSF.

Having defied the ICRC, the 'French doctors' joined their British elders—nurtured by American philanthropy—in an alliance of different traditions and modern humanitarian action began to develop. In France, MSF, MDM, ACF and other NGOs emerged, and took their place alongside Oxfam, Save the Children and CARE. There was no real competition between them: public demand for humanitarian action was strong, crises abounded and states were willingly ceding the responsibility to respond to NGOs, which were becoming more professional and seeing their budgets rise: they were the spearheads of a civil society on the rise.

The fall of the Berlin Wall inaugurated a new configuration of international relations and saw important changes in NGOs. The cards were reshuffled in favour of new alliances, and conflicts changed considerably. Wars of extermination, where the main objective of the combatants is to eliminate a section of the population increased (such as in Rwanda, Bosnia, Kosovo and Darfur): civilians now are the first victims of conflicts. Their form also became increasingly complex. Sometimes a regular army fought a rebel force (as in Sudan, Angola and Sri Lanka); at other times different factions fought each other in a context where the state could no longer contain violence (as in Somalia, Liberia and Sierra Leone). Increasingly, marginal elements (militias, mercenaries, border country troops, mafias) started competing with 'traditional' actors in these conflicts, making alliances more fluid, rules more obscure and the security of humanitarian staff more and more uncertain. These numerous, complex, 'low-intensity' conflicts, as they are sometimes called (such as that in the eastern region of the Democratic Republic of the Congo) often escaped media attention, and NGOs found it difficult to raise the necessary funds for action. In other conflicts, such as Kosovo, Afghanistan and Iraq, the major military and economic powers intervened to eliminate a real or established threat, to defend or establish 'democracy' or to save the population from humanitarian disaster—a disaster that these interventions often provoked or worsened.

Faced with these displays of excessive and over-reported force, humanitarian organisations, whose mandates require them to provide assistance, faced serious difficulties in defining their role, trapped as they were by the dilemma of denouncing or saving lives. The situation brought back to the surface key debates on humanitarian principles, international law on the protection of civil populations and access to war victims. Are humanitarian NGOs still as independent as they would like to believe? Should they agree to be the instruments of states in the name of the superior interests of victim populations, or should they refuse to participate in official mechanisms, at the risk of flouting their mandates?

From the early 1970s to the late 1980s, while states left the humanitarian assistance of populations to international solidarity associations, humanitarian NGOs were the independent soldiers of democracy. Viewed condescendingly by those in power, idolised by the public as the last heroes of a society lacking ideals, humanitarian NGOs played the role of the court fool: the whimsical creature whose job it was to amuse the king, able to tell the truth without fear of punishment as long as he did not question the sovereign's power.

Today, states have decided to take back the initiative and integrate humanitarian action into a wider global reorganisation, of which they hope to be the main artisans. The United States declares that states situated on a mysterious 'Axis of Evil' are pariahs, and launches a war of retaliation in Afghanistan and a 'preventive' war in Iraq. But the United States unfairly gets the blame when, in their wake, many states are following the same policy, but toning it down and keeping a lower profile. What about NGOs in all this? The Bishop's diagonal versus the Axis of Evil...

These problems and many others are widely discussed in the humanitarian community. They all boil down to a single question: what role can or should humanitarian organisations play on the new international geopolitical chessboard? British, American and French humanitarian NGOs differ in their relationship with the state. The former two have always had close relations with their governments, whereas the French put themselves forward as an alternative to state action, which they saw as hostage to the rules of diplomacy. Products of different traditions, but motivated by the same objectives, what is the position of humanitarian organisations at the start of the twenty-first century in the reorganisation of a fragmented world?

The Indian Ocean tsunami in late 2004, a staggering event with worldwide repercussions, sheds light on and still serves as a useful point of reference when beginning to discuss this question. While the conflicts we have listed in Darfur, Sierra Leone, and Liberia. often attract little attention from the media and the public (and therefore donors), what lessons can be learned from the huge surge in solidarity generated by this tsunami?

Without doubt, the brutal and 'natural' character of the event largely contributed to this unprecedented surge. The inevitability attached to it lends it some kind of purity, which undoubtedly made citizens the world over willing to donate freely. All this happened as if the public knew no restraint in this case, whereas they feel suspicious when it comes to helping victims of wars with obviously political causes which are sometimes difficult to explain. In a way this was the painful simplicity of nature, against the ambiguity of human action. The second lesson we can draw from this enormous worldwide reaction is that NGOs appeared to be the obvious, single answer in such a situation.

They appeared as the unarmed and calming force for those people who would have liked to act, but were not able to. On the site of such dramatic events they were, in some way, the advance guard of our conscience which was not completely detached. This is a good lesson, reassuring for thousands of volunteers who embark on humanitarian activities each year. Yet, there is a third lesson: NGOs are also trapped by their own image, and aware that it is regularly tarnished. NGOs have difficulty in making their voices heard and their limitations known. Sometimes, they may even refuse to admit these limitations themselves—to own up to the fact that they are unable to reconstruct a country, torn as they are between the desire to do all they can, and the impulse to admit that they cannot do it all.

This overexposed social subject—the NGO—is also one of the most misunderstood. The main lesson to be drawn from the tsunami is that the public needs to be informed about the reality of NGOs today. Beyond that, the public must reclaim the organisations that they created, understand their strengths and weaknesses, so that they can continue to support them and question them. This book aims to contribute to this process. To help improve our understanding of NGOs, we invited eleven humanitarians and academics, British and French, to reflect on four major current humanitarian problems: The maturity crisis, or how French and British NGOs are responding to the changes they are going through; An assessment of humanitarian action, or how NGOs could become subject to performance criteria; The position of NGOs on the new geopolitical chessboard, or how international solidarity associations fit into global politics; and Humanitarian action and religion, or how the spiritual and the temporal coexist in humanitarian action today.

The authors that have taken part in this book are humanitarians and academics from France and Britain who bring their experience, viewpoint and expectations to bear on each of the four themes. Perhaps for the first time French and Anglo-Saxon humanitarians are in dialogue. A dialogue that we hope will shine precious light on the agreements and differences between these two approaches, which come from distinct traditions in a context where the balance of the world is being reinterpreted.

Far from succumbing to the usual, often ill-founded, criticisms increasingly levelled at humanitarian action, we have adopted Kant's definition of 'critique', as a review by the mind of what it can perceive and understand, in particular, a review carried out by the intellect on its own limitations of reason. Having been involved in the humanitarian action that we are defending, we have no other objective, along with the authors who have accompanied us on this adventure, than to provide an insight into the complexity of another great adventure which started the day a few men and women sided with the damned of this world.

PART 1

THE MATURITY CRISIS

Going back to the birth of MSF, the 'French doctors' adventure has lasted almost forty years. Seen from other side of the Channel and the Atlantic, the mother of French medical NGOs cuts an impertinent young figure next to her Anglo-Saxon counterparts. Yet all of them have been experiencing turbulent times in the last few years; proof that an identity crisis can strike at any age. It also shows that the differences between them are perhaps not as great as they seem. This is what Philippe Ryfman and Hugo Slim explain, refereed by Egbert Sondorp, a researcher, particularly familiar with the mysteries of MSF.

2

CRISES OF MATURITY AND TRANSFORMATION IN FRENCH NGOs

Philippe Ryfman

While the public often ignores it, and they themselves are reluctant to admit it, humanitarian organisations have become complex entities. Like other structures in the same situation, they are going through cyclical crises, regularly reshaping their identity. This is all the more the case as the environment in which they are developing is also changing exponentially every ten years since the end of World War II. At the beginning of the twenty-first century, observing the general context of international humanitarian aid, the American journalist David Rieff argued that 'most humanitarian NGOs seem more inclined to abandon their independence so that they may sit at high table with the leaders of the big powers and the United Nations'.[1] From this he concluded that the end was near for independent non-governmental humanitarian action. In the end, reality refuted this gloomy prediction. However, without going as far, less critical observers speak, to say the least, of a major turning point.

There is no doubt that French NGOs are affected to varying degrees by serious and sudden changes of direction. Their British and American counterparts experience similar changes of course; but historically, the French community of development and humanitarian NGOs has long been strongly divided in comparison to those across the Channel or the other side of the Atlantic Ocean. They were established later and are still greatly influenced by the medical professions. Their more recent trans-nationalisationism, their relationship with the government and their position in society are different. Hence the common tendency is to test the 'French model' against the 'British' or 'American' model (both often characterised in mainland Europe as 'Anglo-Saxon'). The latter being considered to have gradually transformed NGOs into service providers, whereas the former is supposed to continue to favour the political and social aspects of its mandate as well as maintaining a strong not-for-profit capacity relying not only on philanthropy but also on a democratic organisation process. In practice, however, and in the way they have coped with what one could call maturity tests, British, American and French humanitarian NGOs are not today so different, particularly if we consider the answers that these different NGOs communities have brought to the big questions that NGOs are asking themselves.

A Very Specific History

Each NGO community—in the North as in the South—has its own particular history. Its positioning, dimensions and relationship with politics depend on the historical conditions of this development, followed by the degree of international projection and private humanitarian action in a particular country. This is easily demonstrated in the last twenty-five years, with the enlargement of the European Union, and the proliferation of organisations implementing programmes outside their national territory, where no tradition of this kind existed before.

In France, the Enlightenment popularised the notion of 'humanity', and Voltaire became the passionate spokesman of those who were shocked by the failings of the old monarchies faced with the Lisbon earthquake in 1755. But, unlike in Britain, the fight to abolish slavery at the end of the eighteenth and beginning of the nineteenth centuries remained limited to a small intellectual and political circle. Its abolition remained a state matter, and anti-slavery associations never had the same influence as in Britain or the United States. Similarly no French Florence Nightingale emerged from the Crimean war. Nor was there a Clara Barton during the 1871 civil war between legal government seating in Versailles and Parisian uprising, known as 'La Commune'.[2] Admittedly the future national Red Cross Society developed rapidly, but the government's hold remained predominant for a long time.[3] Moreover, it was not born into its current form until 1940 under the aegis—by the way—of the Vichy Regime.[4] While the period following the First World War witnessed new initiatives, these were generally short-lived or politically branded, for example in favour of the young USSR during the famine that followed the civil war. Or Spanish Republic civilians at the end of the thirties. The defeat of France in 1940 obviously did nothing to facilitate the emergence of NGOs aiming to help civilian populations in occupied or newly liberated countries, akin to Oxfam in Britain, or either to CARE or Catholic Relief Services in the US. Nevertheless, before and after the Second World War, colonial propaganda, by highlighting the emblematic figure of the doctor fighting epidemics and the missionary working in the health and education sectors, paradoxically contributed to raising awareness of problems in what we didn't yet call the Third World.

From the 1950s the theme of development aid would be at the origin of a first wave of NGOs, some of whose founders had previously been involved in the fight for decolonisation. On the Catholic Church's initiative, the Comité Catholique Contre la Faim et pour le Développement (CCFD) was established in 1965, the same year as Frères des Hommes (FDH) was founded. A few years later, new organisations would occupy the public and media space; more or less breaking away from their predecessors they would often identify themselves with the generic term 'sans frontiérisme' (i.e. 'without borders').

This neologism, derived from the name of MSF founded in 1971, was to become a great success. These NGOs would be characterised, above all, by the advancement of a set of themes linking speaking out ('witnessing'), sanctification of field work and programme implementation. This operational focus (which was often limited at the beginning) would grow in strength, relying on the gradual professionalisation of the voluntary sector structure, which itself was in search of a real professionalism of action for beneficiary groups. These NGOs would also demonstrate an uncommon aptitude for gaining media coverage and for raising money to pay for their work. From then on they would supplant their predecessors, who continued to favour development projects, in the preferences of both private donors and public backers. If the faith-based NGO CCFD was able to live on, almost all the other development NGOs would see their size diminish and their influence stagnate, if not disappear altogether.

The French public still identify humanitarian NGOs from the stereo-type of the 'French doctor', yet they are all far from being predomi-nantly medical. Organisations such as the formerly Vétérinaires Sans Frontières (VSF)[5] or HI adapted or duplicated the original model. In the following two decades, a third generation of NGOs such as ACF, Solidarités, Première Urgence (PU) or Agence d'Aide à la Coopération Technique Et au Développement (ACTED), rallied to the defence of new categories of target populations, insisting on a combination of professionalism and professionalisation. The end of the Cold War and the collapse of the Soviet bloc produced the same effects in France as in other Western countries: multiplying their fields of action and rein-forcing existing organisations working in human rights, development and, characteristically for France, humanitarian issues. These changes also provoked regular creation of new organisations in France. The fight against the impunity of those responsible for massive acts of vio-lence in the name of ethnic cleansing (after the experiences in Bosnia and Rwanda); access to civil populations—that had become major strategic stakes in armed conflicts; fights against malnutrition, land-mines, the pandemic of HIV/Aids and other endemic diseases; the expansion of micro credit; taking care of street children and crisis prevention; and lastly, ecology, would all became major areas of activity.

Having reached maturity during the first decade of the century, the French humanitarian movement is, nevertheless, at the end of it, devel-oping a watershed moment.

Multi-Faceted Crises

A threefold phenomenon—not exclusive to France—is unfolding. NGOs confront a crisis in terms of financial resources, legitimacy and humanitarian space. As mentioned above, these problems do not come out of the blue and the organisations concerned have acquired un-doubted experience which seems to equip them better to face up to them.

Financial Resources

Financial resources first: several large organisations (HI, MDM and ACF) have experienced financial problems since the beginning of the new millennium. Access to private and public funds operates in an extremely competitive environment. NGOs have found it difficult to acquire new donors and gain their loyalty. Despite the momentum it triggered at the time, the Asian tsunami of 26 December 2004 scarcely contributed to a long-term increase in the number of donors. The consequences of the economic and financial crisis which exploded in autumn 2008 could turn out to be in the future a problem for certain NGOs. But for the moment, that is not the case: all French major humanitarian NGOs have increased their resources in 2009. They are still receiving important new donations, following Haiti's earthquake of 12 January 2010, even if this is less than for the tsunami.

Human Resources

Amongst medium and large French NGOs, professionalisation, which has long been regarded with suspicion, is now an established fact.[6] Of course, for some, the worry remains that a salaried layer will be created, living off NGOs by taking away grants and which could also risk taking power away from the activists.[7] Normative questions tend to figure most on today's agenda: questions of remuneration; career development and the differing status of international (or 'expatriates') staff, including volunteers. As in the UK and the USA, paid staff, who for a long time were in the minority,[8] can progress quickly today and have become more and more the standard also for French humanitarian workers, as explained below.

However, there is also a clear gap between the number of positions available and the potential recruitment pool. The whole French NGO community (humanitarian aid and development aid) still offers limited career openings. In 2005, the humanitarian and development sectors employed 2,232 full time paid staff on French territory, as well as 4,603 *bénévoles* (unpaid volunteers), 367 interns and fifty-six *volontaires* (volunteers who received an allowance and are accorded some legal rights). Around 4,500 'expatriates' (paid, *bénévoles*, *volontaires* and some interns) were working out in the field.[9] Much precisely, regarding some major NGOs in 2007, MSF-F headquarters in Paris counted 130 employees, while around 400 international staff and 4100 national staff worked in the field. For MDM-F, figures are respectively 210 (HQ + regional offices on French territory), 180 and 1300. And for ACF-F, 137, 300 and 2500.

It remains that staff recruitment—particularly for technical and specialist posts, is difficult—specifically because of the skills, experience and culture of humanitarian commitment expected by these NGOs; this is also the case when turning to local staff, whose competencies are often equal, if not superior, to those recruited in the North.

The lack of human resources in the field makes the management of increasingly heavy and complex operations particularly difficult, even where they have secured funding from public or private sources. The crisis in Darfur at the start of the decade is a good example. Whatever the seemingly high number of international personnel deployed in the west of Sudan in some years might suggest—over a hundred for MSF-F, more than fifty for ACF-F, for example—in reality these NGOs have been afflicted with serious difficulties in recruiting both specialists and experienced and competent managers. This has not been helped by the expulsion by President al Bashir's government in March 2009 of thirteen international NGOs. Staff turnover is high and some of these posts can remain vacant for months at a time.

Legitimacy

The fact that NGOs are overvalued in today's world has its downside, in France as elsewhere: their legitimacy is often called into question. NGOs are criticised by politicians, the media and researchers,[10] arguing, amongst other things that they have not been democratically elected and tend to be 'self legitimating'.

For this reason, the legitimacy of NGOs is all the more likely 'to crumble and become damaged'[11] as their mandates expand. The identification of what constitutes the heart of this mandate (that which is specific to the NGO) or its evolution becomes a key element. The notion of NGO governance now also represents a major challenge.[12] Like companies before them, humanitarian NGOs find themselves facing stringent questions about their *modus operandi*, their management, their possible lack of democracy, their employment costs and how they balance the views of stakeholders. Furthermore, some have noticed the return in force of States on the international scene; this could lead to NGOs having their power restricted to that which States would be willing to allow them[13] and creates a feeling of unease.

Humanitarian Space

The worldwide humanitarian community is currently facing other worrying questions: in war zones—particularly the so-called non-international conflicts, such as civil wars, guerrilla conflicts and militia warfare—the impartiality and indeed the very presence of external actors are increasingly challenged by local players. Another problem NGOs face is the presence of foreign armies—notably Western ones—in war-torn regions. For example, French NGOs in Afghanistan—as well as their British or American colleagues—expect to be refused access to victims, deportation, the risk of exploitation of aid and the rapid degradation of security conditions (muggings, kidnappings, incarceration, assassinations). In other words, the existence of an autonomous humanitarian space enabling needs assessments, non-discriminatory aid and monitoring and evaluation of impact is questioned. This leads to increasing doubt—from Sri Lanka to Afghanistan, Pakistan to Burma/Myanmar or Darfur to Somalia—as to the meaning, scope and acceptability of humanitarian action. These doubts are given greater weight by the fact that one of the major characteristics of private humanitarian organisations is their internal capacity for self-questioning. They have a strong tradition of permanently questioning their actions and of often fierce internal debate (for example on the opening or closing of a programme). This self-questioning capacity reaches a high level in French NGOs community. As a result, in Afghanistan for instance, French NGOs mostly are very critical against what they consider the international coalition strategy, regarding humanitarian aid as a pacification element. And they turn down any involvement in Provincial Reconstruction Team (PRT) system.

Meeting the Challenges

Far from remaining inactive in the face of these very real problems, French NGOs have reacted strongly to the three challenges described above. However, other questions trouble them.

Financial Resources

Contrary to persistent public belief, most NGO funding in France does not depend on the government. This is worlds apart from the British and American context where NGOs are dependent to a greater degree on public funding, by the UK's Department for International Development (DFID), or the United States Agency for International Development (USAID). As far as humanitarian relief is concerned, civil society may assert itself strongly, yet granting aid is not a priority for politicians.

So, French NGOs are mainly funded by the private sector, with only a small proportion of their funding coming from Official Development Assistance (ODA). Regular surveys that have been carried out since 1986 confirm this statistically. The most recent, carried out in 2004 and 2005, draws on data concerning a panel of 400 NGOs, 159 of which responded directly to a specially put together questionnaire—practically all those with at least some national recognition and scale. The budgets in question were divided into nine bands, ranging from those of over €100m to the smallest at under €40,000. The study showed that in 2005, (of the total percentage of public resources of the NGOs studied), the share of direct state funding was only 21 per cent with a 4.8 per cent contribution from local and regional governments.[14] On the other hand, international public funding continues to expand. From 1991 to 2005 it increased from 56 per cent of the total to 76.7 per cent, making a global increase of €158.26m. Nevertheless, in 2005, the public resources of French NGOs in the sector came to no more than 36 per cent of the total of their financial resources. In other words, private funding is clearly the most significant at 64 per cent. Moreover, the ratio of public to private funding is astonishingly stable. In 1991 it was at the very similar ratio of 35/65.[15]

In short, the share of ODA going to NGOs is in France around only 1.2 per cent, while it reaches 7 per cent in Great Britain and between 30 to 50 per cent in USA.

In 2005, French development and humanitarian NGOs again reported having spent 72.8 per cent of their resources on the ground to finance their operations. In addition, 8.7 per cent of resources were used to cover fundraising costs and 7.3 per cent on carrying out their activities in France, of which about half was spent on educating about international development (awareness raising amongst the general public). Organisational running costs average about 10–11 per cent of their budget but make up a lower percentage (around 6–7 per cent) when emergency action is being undertaken.[16]

It is clear from this that French NGOs have been diversifying their funding. As a result, their individual funding profile is highly varied. Thus then, and in 2009,[17] MSF-F had a 94 per cent private funding ratio with a total amount of €174.6m, HI-F was at 53.2 per cent with an amount of €100.9m, and MDM-F at 59 per cent with an amount of

€60.6m. On the other hand ACF-F showed a reverse ratio with 40 per cent private funding and 55 per cent public and a total of €80m, PU declared almost 100 per cent public funding, and ACTED 95 per cent.

Trying to stabilise these resources has proved, and will continue to prove to be a key factor in the future of French NGOs. In this respect, efforts have been made in various directions by some organisations. For private funds, French NGOs are looking at the British practice of rallying new supporters to the humanitarian cause. Since 2004, street fundraising techniques that had long been used in the UK have been introduced in France. These involve convincing passers-by, particularly young people, to sign up to direct debit payments. ACF-F, MSF-F, HI-F, MDM-F or CARE-F (French branch of this US-born NGO) are currently exploiting this market widely. The unexpected birth of online donations in early 2005, a consequence of the Indian Ocean tsunami, has also been carefully examined by finance officials, who are asking themselves whether this is a temporary phenomenon linked to that event, or a lasting tendency, particularly among young people. Nevertheless as far as 2008, its impact on NGO budgets remains limited. But things have begun to change since 2009. A legislative reform at the start of the decade—initially targeted at cultural patronage—seems also to have produced beneficial and unexpected benefits in the humanitarian sector, however these are difficult to quantify both in terms of the volume of donations from private individuals and a significant increase in company contributions.[18] In any case, the government has significantly raised tax benefits to both private donors (the taxable ceiling for donations increased to 20 per cent and the level of tax reduction increased to 66 per cent and in certain cases 75 per cent with a possibility to delay payment for up to five years) and to companies (60 per cent deduction on gifts from taxable profits with a limit of five donations for each 1,000 of turnover). This system is the most favourable for non profit organisations among all the members of European Union.

Partnerships between business and NGOs have also expanded a great deal in the last ten years. This has come despite on the one hand the humanitarian sector attracting less interest from companies than anything to do with the environment or global warming. And on the other hand part of NGOs elites keep a certain mistrust towards commercial companies' real aims. Finally, several medium and large French NGOs have watched the emergence of alternative and significant funders with interest. Firstly, private funding is offered by new and powerful philanthropic foundations, along the model of The Bill & Melinda Gates Foundation in the USA, or those created by company Chief Executives in emerging countries. Then, regarding public funds, a strategy of long-term humanitarian finance on the ground is being led by new funder countries, above all the oil rich countries, such as Qatar. MDM-F has recently opened a bureau there, with the additional objective of increasing acceptance of a Western NGOs in the Arab/ Muslim world. But MSF-F has been there before by opening an office in United Arab Emirates at Abu Dhabi in the nineties. Put in stand-by after 9/11, it has been now reactivated.

Regarding international public funding, the sole-contributor model, which eventually led to the disappearance of NGOs such as Equilibre and Medicus Mundi, has become an exception. Although the European Union remains the main funder, medium and large French NGOs have become expert at requesting subsidies from foreign governments, in addition to the funding provided by the United Nations. Thus, Britain's DFID contributes to the funding of programmes led by NGOs such as HI-F, ACF-F or MDM-F. And USAID contributes to ACF-F, ACTED, PU and others.

Finally, at national level, under the presidency of Jacques Chirac, the state politically proclaimed its desire to see the amount of ODA given to NGOs progressively reach the European average of 5 per cent with an intermediary step to 3 per cent expected in 2007. In terms of figures that should have meant a leap from €71m in 2004 to €258m in 2007, but these commitments have not been respected. Since President Nicolas Sarkozy came to power, the situation has stayed frozen. In 2008 the total French budget for ODA (all sectors taken together) was already no more than €7.27bn. It is also likely that the financial and economic crisis that has been felt since autumn 2008 will chip away further at the government share of public funding for French NGOs, which is already limited as previously shown. In October 2008 Oxfam's French branch (OXFAM-France, Agir Ici)[19] revealed a government project of budget cuts worth several hundred million euros to the fight against poverty in sub-Saharan Africa. The government denied this but drastic cuts seem to have taken place in public subsidies intended for health programmes. In this context and without a major strategic change in favour of French NGOs from l'Agence Française de Développement (AFD)—the pivotal operator of French development aid which also tends to take charge of humanitarian aid in post-crisis and post-conflict contexts—or in political will, it is very unlikely that the share of national public finance in NGOs' resources will progress very much in years to come.

Where staff are concerned, the crucial question of developing professional career paths in the private aid sector, even if some hesitate to class them as such, is less and less of a taboo. Though some analysts[20] continue to think that, 'for members of NGOs, humanitarian work is not a stage in a career path but mark a moment in a voluntary commitment', professional pathways in the NGO community are now quite easy to detect, and are already the subject of research.[21]

Indeed, how can voluntary workers be persuaded to work long-term for the humanitarian cause if they are not offered a minimal level of financial security and the possibility of development, progression, vocational training and work-life balance? While some improvements have been noted in the posts of Co-ordinator, Head of Mission and Administrator, NGOs still find it difficult to retain certain specific technical skills. Even without considering it from the commercial or public point of view, the attraction of higher salaries, better living conditions and clearer career prospects outside the sector can work against the French humanitarian sector. Besides, exit from the sector is harder in France than—for instance—in UK. It is not so easy to work for commercial companies and nearly impossible to become a national civil servant, regarding specific French process of recruitment for Civil service.

The fact that international staff[22] were not generally paid workers but managed under a special status ('volontaires') has differentiated French NGOs from their British and American counterparts for a long time. Since 2003, however, (as previously noted) the salary system has developed in a spectacular way (at ACF-F, HI-F, MDM-F and MSF-F in particular), and a law governing voluntary work has finally been passed.[23] This clarifies the modalities and maximum duration of voluntary work, and should contribute to its definition and accelerate the development of a more stable, long-term employment framework for international workers.

However the level of pay, even if it has increased in an attempt to attract and retain the necessary skills, remains lower than that offered by Anglo Saxon NGOs. Thus in 2007, the gross average monthly wage of the ten highest paid staff of ACF-F rose to €4,660, with the average salary being €2,735. In the field, 65.5 per cent of the international workforce were still enlisted under the status of *volontariat de solidarité internationale* (VSI)—then governed by the law of 23 February 2005—and received a total monthly allowance of between €838 and €1,143 Payment of staff has progressed spectacularly; 34.5 per cent of overseas workers are now paid (Heads of Mission, Co-ordinators, Administrators and experts), compared to just 8 per cent in 2002. They receive a gross monthly payment of between €1,550 and €2,450. At MSF-F the highest gross salaries vary between €5,134 and €6,150 per month. In the field, international staff salaries are increasing. For MDM-F the highest gross salary peaks at €7,274, with the average being €2,604 and the lowest, €1,469. So a part of French international humanitarian workers continue to have the status of *volontaires* with (VSI or with no status at all if they leave for a very short period), but here too—as said—payment for their work is advancing.[24] For the smallest NGOs the amounts are markedly smaller. Probably the category of *volontaires* will not vanish, because a large part of French humanitarian NGOs attached a value to it, especially for short—term missions and also for a first experience in the field.

But this peculiar situation has consequences: a classical French humanitarian worker's career will often begin by working first in a French NGO as a volunteer, then by becoming salaried. After three to five years the pattern is to usually quit the French humanitarian community for an American, British, Australian or Canadian NGO.

Legitimacy

Based on the self-legitimising process mentioned above, NGOs must also establish their long-term legitimacy. In order to do so, various standards (the demonstration of operational capacity, expertise, capacity to mobilise and lobby, the level of anchorage within civil society and legal recognition) can be useful[25] in building legitimacy and ensuring its durability. They would also gain from being more representative. Without wishing to copy the social system of salaried workers' trade unions, such an approach would open up new opportunities, even more so if it were linked to the theme of participatory democracy, which is supported, to some extent, by public opinion around the anti-globalisation movement.

Humanitarian Space

NGOs alone cannot contribute to the recognition, maintenance and viability of humanitarian space. Civil societies, international organisations (beginning with the United Nations), the European Union and governments must also play their part in this However, NGOs are not wholly devoid of power: they can put pressure on other actors on the humanitarian scene and more broadly at international level so as to, directly or indirectly, put retrospective power on local protagonists.

The option of a spectacular retreat from a given territory constitutes a choice, as does the maintenance of a discrete presence, but is by no means a panacea that can always be reproduced. The departure of MSF-F from Afghanistan in July 2004 triggered a similar reaction in other French humanitarian organisations which had also been there for a long time. In 2008, ACF-F quit Sri-Lanka and Burundi after murders of national and international staff workers.

One can expect assessments of the reduction of humanitarian space to be different, as there is no general theory of operational capability on the ground. Each situation must be analysed according to parameters specific to each NGO programme and local, regional and international context. This approach has been adopted by organisations such as HI-F, ACF-F, CARE-F and Solidarités. The emphasis is more frequently on resorting to advocacy to obtain access to victims or to avoid as far as possible the exploitation of aid. Here again, the similarity between the French and British approaches is evident. Nevertheless, although NGOs have tackled the problems head-on, new challenges are already appearing, amongst the most important of which are transnationalisation and critical mass.

Emergence of Faith-Based NGOs

Faith-based NGOs exist in the development aid sector in France and some are very strong like CCFD or Secours-Catholique (French name for Caritas-F). But it was almost not the case in the humanitarian sector. Things seem to have moved around over the past five years, and consequently faith-based humanitarian NGOs have begun to emerge. A characteristic example is the one of Secours Islamique-F, French branch of trans-national NGO Islamic Relief. Funded by French muslim donors their resources in 2009 were around €20m. With a 95 per cent ratio of private funding which has doubled in only one year (2008/2009). This new phenomenon will be under scrutiny in the future.

Trans-Nationalisation and 'Critical Mass'

Through a network of sister NGOs or branches, some NGOs have become truly trans-national. Thus they tend to make up true trans-national NGO networks which have the capacity to project and deploy considerable resources, as well as having outposts in a large number of 'civil societies' both in the North and the South. Amongst British agencies, in particular Oxfam and Save the Children Fund, these choices were made a long time ago. In France MSF-F has also initiated a trans-national NGO network, which has acquired a strong capacity for international projection and synergy, despite its highly decentralised operation. MDM-F, ACF-F and HI-F are at various stages of network-building. This phenomenon was accompanied by a parallel survey by a researcher, Viviane Tchernonog of the Matisse laboratory at the Centre National de la Recherche Scientifique (CNRS) and the University Paris I. Published in 2007, this demonstrated that 40,000 organisations in France described themselves as 'humanitarian' in 2006—double the number compared to the previous survey, which reported on the year 2000.[26] Yet the allocation of this humanitarian label seems to have gone too far and does not reflect the reality of NGOs that are truly engaged in humanitarian action and aid projects in developing countries. The number of NGOs actually active in this field is, instead, estimated at around 500. To compare with the total number of non-profit organisations, which—in France—is around 900,000 (1,400,000 in USA and 170,000 in UK). So, for France, it is impossible to scientifically determine an accurate figure and even this kind of estimate is probably fictitious in part; only a few dozen NGOs have real operational capability diversified across several projects. Small or micro-NGOs set up across the regions in France are, in any case, difficult to quantify, and understanding their real aim is difficult.

From then on, the question of 'critical mass' gradually becomes a real issue. Medium and large NGOs are faced with programmes that are increasingly costly in terms of financial and human resources and management. The demands of large humanitarian missions may require strengthening the management of the field team by recruiting expatriates solely for that task. This requires adequate financial resources and skilled staff. The total expatriate and national staff deployed by ACF-F in Darfur in 2005 (over 1,000) greatly exceeded staff at its Paris head-quarters (100 at that moment). Management control, strict monitoring of expenditure at headquarters and in the field, enhancement of tele-communications, management of teams by human resource specialists are all constantly on the agenda. Not to mention inspections by the Cour des Comptes (National Court of Accounts) which has the power to monitor non-for-profit organisations raising private funds. And also various administrative inspection bodies which, along with public funders (such as the European Community Humanitarian Office [ECHO])[27], currently require sophisticated tax liability procedures and internal control as well as extra staff for their implementation and interface functions.

NGOs have several options, including self-limitation, the 'niche' effect and internal or external growth. Without going into detail, inter-nal growth does not necessarily mean an increase in size, but question-ing, for example, the very content of action. In this regard, British (and Irish) initiatives are being closely observed. Some of these NGOs (Goal, Concern and Merlin) are no longer afraid of addressing the sensitive question of closing programmes to concentrate more resources on fewer, better-selected countries. In France, the subject is still largely taboo: a strategy of opening missions in as many places as possible remains a key element, and closure is a difficult process[28] for the man-agement of certain NGOs, worried about offering their opponents an opportunity.

Other options are also too much neglected. For example, the mutu-alisation of NGOs which are equivalent in size and whose programmes complement each other nationally could lead to strong partnerships and economies of scale.[29] The Europeanisation of NGOs is also cur-rently lacking, on the pretext that there is no European legal associa-tion status. In reality, the European space has been taken into account for a long time, above all in the case of the co-financing awarded by Brussels to European Union NGOs and the development of community NGOs at European level (such as Concord and Voice). Till very recent years, there were no real strategies in France similar to that of Oxfam, which in recent years transformed the Dutch Novib into Oxfam-Neth-erlands and Intermon in Spain into Oxfam-España. The pooling of interests that was initiated in 2004 between Oxfam and the French NGO Agir Ici led to the same result, with its integration into Oxfams's network in 2006 so that it became Oxfam-France Agir Ici. But the initiative came from Great Britain. The extension of CARE's network with the opening of CARE-France, was rather similar. By comparison World Vision International (WVI) also tried to open a branch in Paris ('Vision Mondiale'), but until now the result is limited.

Renewal of the Ruling Elites

Finally, some French NGOs, specifically the major players, face the difficulty of renewing their leadership. In the case of managers and CEO, some (even if they are small in number), have occupied the highest posts for twenty, sometimes thirty years. So replacing them with a new generation has presented some difficulties. But now the take over has been largely done. It is much harder, however, to find candidates to sit on governing boards which, in France, are elected and not co-opted, with steep legal liabilities for members. This leaves NGOs open to the risk of becoming insular.

Essentially, if French NGOs manage these challenges successfully, it will mean that they have reached maturity. In order to maximise their chances of doing so, they would certainly gain from comparing their viewpoints with their British and American colleagues and analysing successes and failures. Work could focus on building common areas of discussion and exchange. The unquestionable strengthening of functional and institutional links between national NGO co-ordinators in recent years represents a first advance in this respect. Relations between British Overseas NGOs for Development (BOND) and Co-ordination Solidarité Urgence Développement (SUD) were distinctly strengthened in this way. Symbolic direct cross channel connections between NGOs are, on the other hand, still flimsy and, above all, limited. Paradoxically links are, somewhere, stronger and closer with the US NGOs community, particularly between central co-ordination, InterAction and SUD.

Some partnerships have, however, already proved themselves, either in international campaigns such as those led by Oxfam and MSF-F or HI-F and the Mines Advisory Group (MAG), or in field operations, where MSF, ACF, Oxfam, SCF, HI and Merlin practice operational partnerships and exchanges in numerous places across the globe. Yet here too opportunities do not seem to be sufficiently capitalised upon.

The aim is not to deny the existence of particularities, such as differences of approach and function between the French, and British NGO communities. In general (as illustrated here), such differences are probably fewer than those that exist between them and American NGOs—throughout the Bush administration in any case—in matters such as the relationship with politics, field staff security and relations with the military. All the more so as in France a number of NGOs have equally, begun to practice[30] a multi-faceted and multi-mandate strategy, combining development programmes, humanitarian missions, advocacy on global governance and involvement in environmental preservation and the fight against global warming.

The development of a methodology aimed at structuring future Franco-British (and perhaps Franco-American) involvement more solidly would be a quickly attainable objective.[31] This vast project would also have the merit of going beyond rather sterile debates, such as whether or not NGOs are the bearers of values.[32] Even without non-governmental agencies in the field, there would still certainly be something named humanitarian action. But it would lack the contours, the standing and the influence to which assist vulnerable or suffering populations. That strength and effectiveness are due precisely to the existence of the non-governmental component which preservation is for victims of armed conflicts or natural disasters the central point, whatever the NGOs concerned.

3

ESTABLISHMENT RADICALS

AN HISTORICAL OVERVIEW OF BRITISH NGOS

Hugo Slim

Like most human enterprises, NGOs are formed in that exhilarating moment when a few determined people sit around a table and say 'we've got to do something about this'. An idea usually follows. Sometimes this idea makes it out of the room and struggles into life, occasionally growing into something very large and effective.

The so-called voluntary sector in British society has a long tradition of such people, such rooms, such meetings, such ideas and much success. Yet, for every idea that worked, hundreds of others have probably failed or remained relatively small. For at least two centuries there has been considerable social and political value placed on charitable entrepreneurs, and there still is.[1] Successful charities and their leaders are admired in British society. 'Doing good' is recognised as impressive partly because it shows initiative and partly because it is often slightly subversive and challenges the status quo.

But there is also a strong Puritanical streak in the contemporary British approach to charity. The British like their charities to be gently rebellious and independent, but essentially respectable. Above all, they like charities to be practical and constructive with money going very obviously to the people who need it. They also like their charities to be savvy and effective communicators but never to be flash. This particular British approach to charities has long been encapsulated in law. UK Charity law strikes a balance between charity and politics in a trade-off that gives charities protection from tax and excessive government control in return for protecting politicians from direct attack from potentially partisan and unelected charities. This accommodation enables British charities to be innovative and challenging but never explicitly confrontational along party lines. They can pursue political activities but can never exist simply to be political.[2]

Happily, this practical, puritan and polite approach also seems to find much in common with the style and temper of the exciting new wave of international Islamic charities in Britain today. In this sense, many of the new international Islamic NGOs which have been founded recently in cities like Birmingham, Bradford, Leicester, Manchester and London are emerging as very British as well as very Islamic. Hopefully, this bodes well for an evolving tradition of international British NGOs that will be made yet stronger from insights and social networks from Islam and other new communities in the UK.

Thus the purpose of this chapter is to present a brief historical overview of the evolution to date of Britain's international NGO sector and to identify a number of key challenges that British NGOs have faced in the last sixty years in particular. In so doing, I hope to reveal a distinct British tradition and a consistently pragmatic approach to problem-solving in British NGOs.

British Activism in the Nineteenth Century

As one might expect, class has played a significant role in the development of British NGOs. Historically, Britain's social entrepreneurs have often been working class people working with extraordinary zeal and energy through trades unions, mutual societies, religious groups and co-operatives. But Britain also has a powerful tradition of middle and upper class social entrepreneurs. It is these people who have tended to found what came to be called 'charities' under British law—commonly known as NGOs today. It is from within this more affluent and privileged tradition that most British international NGOs have emerged. Oxfam, Save the Children, Christian Aid, CAFOD, ActionAid and more recently Merlin, Scottish European Aid, Islamic Relief and Muslim Aid are the result of exceptional middle or upper class vision and energy, often lead by maverick entrepreneurial figures with close ties to particular parts of the British establishment whether left or right, religious or secular, commercial or professional.

In the eighteenth and nineteenth centuries, British society spawned an extraordinary wave of these upper and middle class 'reformers' or 'philanthropists'. Famous names like Elizabeth Fry, William Wilberforce, Florence Nightingale and Lord Shaftesbury were but the tip of the iceberg of a mass of people working in voluntary charitable associations that aimed to transform social attitudes and behaviour on matters such as public education, social housing, public health, the abolition of slavery, the regulation of child labour, women's suffrage, temperance, prostitution and international Christian mission to the millions of 'lost souls' throughout the British empire.

These determined and well-connected figures built surprisingly broad-based social movements around their chosen causes. Typically, they would select patrons and governing boards made up of what the British call 'the great and the good'. These included royalty, aristocracy, bishops, industrialists, bankers and newspaper people as well as eminent persons from the various medical, legal, military, engineering or academic professions relevant to their particular cause. Moving outwards through British society, these nineteenth century prototype NGO activists then set up local networks of support groups throughout Britain's villages, towns and cities which often spread beyond traditional barriers of class.

In addition to the class, social position and personal dynamism of its leading lights, two other social factors were critical to the astonishing development of Britain's voluntary sector in the nineteenth century—women and evangelicalism.

At a time when British public life made little room for women, the voluntary sector provided a unique social and political space for women to be acceptably active in wider society. A massive part of the energy, networking, imagination and hard grind of the British voluntary sector came from women of all classes and it continues to do so. Intelligent upper and middle class ladies at last found a public space in which to be the equal of men. They set up working groups, chaired meetings, addressed assemblies, visited the poor and lobbied the influential husbands of their friends. Working class women were similarly able to be active—time permitting—and also to address and attend meetings. It was usually women who built the genuine social relations between classes that were so important in these social movements.

Another critical factor was the phenomenal spread of evangelical Protestant Christianity across British society. In the nineteenth century, Evangelicalism spread throughout the mainstream Anglican Church to great effect. It was also the guiding spirit of the Calvinist Church of Scotland, the non-conformist churches like the Methodists and Baptists as well as the many smaller chapel groupings in Wales and England. Roman Catholics and Anglo-Catholics were also full of good works at this time but it was the Evangelicals who had a real grip on power. The overwhelming individual experience of conversion and personal salvation that this form of Christianity involved reached across all parts of British society and provided extraordinary impetus to British social movements.

Evangelicalism was deeply activist. Large parts of Britain's Victorian voluntary sector drew on electrifying levels of religious enthusiasm to bring about a better world. Evangelicals did good work because it was God's will and they were enthused and guided by the Holy Spirit to do so. The fact that one was 'born again' and had become 'serious' also meant that a Lord and a miner could find something in common which transcended British social barriers to bind them in a common cause as well as a certain mutual affection and respect.[3]

Even if one was not religious in this way, the activist style of Evangelical Christianity set a tone to charity work and campaigning that many religiously moderate or secular movements emulated and still do. In Britain today, being an activist in Oxfam's trade campaign or the inter-agency arms control campaign requires a sort of spiritual possession and commitment in the tradition of activist evangelicalism. Today one has to be 'passionate' about poverty, trade justice, arms control and so forth. Passion is the great middle class word of early twenty-first century British NGOs—secular and religious alike. If one had to be born again as serious and committed in nineteenth century Britain, one has to be born again as passionate today. It must continue as something of a mystery to our continental European cousins that we British can seem so cold blooded in important personal matters of romance and cuisine while so hot-blooded around good causes.

Colonial Legacy

Another important tributary that has fed the current flow of British NGOs is the history of colonial administration that was such a central part of British imperialism for two hundred and fifty years. In the twentieth century the earlier imperial practice of military rule developed into the more complicated practice of well-intentioned and progressive social administration that tried to introduce modern education, health, agricultural and industrial method to improve the lives of people in British colonies throughout Africa, Asia and the Middle East.

Between 1920–1960 in particular, the Colonial Service contained many idealistic people intent on delivering better public services alongside many Christian missionaries and pro-independence activists who were similarly motivated. In the UK, several centres of excellence emerged around universities and hospitals like London, Liverpool, Edinburgh, Manchester, Oxford, Cambridge and Sussex that specialised in the new disciplines of tropical agriculture, tropical veterinary science, tropical medicine, public health, mass literacy, local governance and, of course, anthropology. These disciplines became highly developed and were then re-framed as the foundation of what became development studies in the 1960s. With the end of Colonialism, many of the more idealistic members of the Colonial Service moved seamlessly into the British Government's new Overseas Development Administration or into UN agencies and British NGOs.

There was a similar cross-fertilisation between British colonial military service and the humanitarian and development sector. A significant number of officers who had seen military service in British counter-insurgency operations around independence struggles in places like Malaya, Kenya, Cyprus, Oman, Aden and Northern Ireland went on to join British NGOs as field officers, executives or Board members. Joining an NGO was a natural way to extend their skills into good works while maintaining a similarly exotic profession.

The legacy from the scientific, political and military expertise of Colonial Administration made a real impression on British NGOs in a key period between 1970 and 1985. For example, a number of Oxfam's first Field Directors in South Asia were former colonial administrators. Similarly, when I joined Save the Children in 1983, the Director-General was ex-Colonial Service and three out of the four international Directors were ex-military officers. The colonial legacy brought with it a particular approach. It favoured working with governments. It instinctively thought strategically across whole sectors like health, education and agriculture. It recognised people's political empowerment and participation as central in taking control of their destiny. It prioritised primary services (like rural clinics or primary schools) over secondary and tertiary ones (like hospitals and universities). It was pragmatic rather than idealistic. It did not distinguish easily between relief and development but realised that poor people's lives were always politically and environmentally precarious so had to be supported in the round not in one area alone. Finally, it placed great value on knowing the country and its key people—on good intelligence and good contacts.

The Two World Wars

If most nineteenth and early twentieth century British activism concerned domestic social issues, imperial mission and colonial rights, the two world wars of the first half of the twentieth century thrust the whole question of war and rapid expeditionary relief into the very centre of an already mature domestic voluntary sector. Both world wars elicited a strong humanitarian response from within British society and produced three large NGOs which remain at the forefront of British internationalism—Save the Children Fund (SCF), Oxfam and Christian Aid. Each of these continued the tradition of entrepreneurial, radical but well connected establishment activism.

Save the Children sprang from World War I and was founded in 1919 by a group of upper and middle class British people—of Liberal hue—who were deeply shocked by the massive civilian suffering caused by the continuing Allied blockade against Germany and Austria. In particular, they were horrified by the suffering of children whose innocence was beyond question. More generally, they regarded the punitive blockade (which today we would call sanctions) as inhumane, unjust and politically short-sighted. A group of politicians, artists and business people formed around the significant charisma and energy of Eglantyne Jebb, the highly intelligent social-worker daughter of a well-off Shropshire family. But, interestingly and typically, Save the Children found cross-class support in Britain and received its most generous early donation from the Union of Coal Miners.

After its early work in Austria and Germany, SCF lead a massive and politically controversial relief effort in the middle of the Russian civil war in 1921, still equally determined to challenge the idea of 'enemy children'. This was perhaps the prototype of the modern, secular, expatriate-led humanitarian relief operation complete with an aggressive fundraising campaign and advocacy strategy at home.[4]

Since this controversial beginning, SCF has remained at the heart of the British establishment and worked in many of the major wars and famines of the last eighty-five years. Alongside its relief programmes, it has always pursued a policy of influencing social, economic, military and political policy in the best interests of children.

The Second World War produced Oxfam, which as the Oxford Committee for Famine Relief was one of the many local committees set up around Britain to challenge the allied Blockade of Nazi Occupied Europe in the Second World War. Oxfam's founders were highly respectable Anglican priests, Oxford academics, Quakers and businessmen. In 1942, the Churchill government refused to lift the blockade for a civilian relief programme but Oxfam did eventually succeed in sending food and clothing via ICRC to victims of the Greek famine in 1943. From this moment on, Oxfam never stopped working—usually preferring to work through local partner organisations but later developing an unmatched expertise in emergency water and sanitation work.

In the Nigerian civil war, the Bangladesh war, the Cambodian war and the Ethiopian famine, Oxfam developed its role as an outspoken advocate for civilian populations, unafraid of criticising political abuse or neglect around wartime suffering. It has continued this practice of humanitarian advocacy ever since. With its intellectual Oxford roots, Oxfam has also always been determined to explore and reveal the structural causes underlying human poverty and suffering. Its significant investment in policy and campaigning has made it the world's market leader in campaigning NGOs.

Another part of the establishment—Britain's Anglican Bishops and their non-conformist counterparts—formed Christian Aid at the end of World War II to prove the importance of the impartial humanitarian ethic in war and of healing after violent conflict. Like Oxfam and Save the Children, in the last sixty years Christian Aid has grown to become one of the UK's largest international NGOs. And, like them, it also sits at the heart of the British establishment—this time a religious one—at once radical, rooted, well connected and respectable. As well as consolidating the NGO sector within the British establishment, the two world wars also put war, the humanitarian ethic and the protection of civilians at the centre of British NGO concerns. Suffering in war would be something that British NGOs would always care about but it would by no means be the only thing that they would care about.

Development and its Tensions

Like their nineteenth and early twentieth century predecessors, most late twentieth century British NGOs were exercised about the full range of human suffering and their interest was not just in individuals as victims but in improving society as a whole. In other words, their sense of mission extended beyond present suffering to future happiness. They were not only motivated by mercy but also by wider social goals. And, like their missionary and colonial forebears, their concerns did not stop at British borders. They had feelings and ideas for the whole world. In agency jargon, they were multi-mandate not single-mandate organisations. They were interested in social progress as well as temporary relief.

With the end of European colonialism in the 1960s, Britain's traditional imperial project of colonial administration, mission and philanthropy was re-framed as something called Development. John F. Kennedy's famous speech and Pope Paul VI's landmark document, Progressio Populi, built on President Truman's post-war doctrine to herald the new era of international development. This would see NGOs playing a leading role in re-defining poverty as 'under-development' and re-naming the colonies as 'the third world' caught in grinding poverty between the competing first and second worlds of the Cold War confrontation.[5] British NGOs engaged in earnest with this re-framing of the world. While emergency relief operations remained important to the values, profile and income of British NGOs, the real priority in-house was to join the struggle against under-development and oppression. NGO focus turned to an analysis and engagement with the political, social and economic structures that shaped poverty and inequality. Much was made of the need to address the causes rather than the symptoms of poverty.

So it was that, in the 1970s, international British charities became 'development agencies'. Many of the new generation of people in British NGOs read Marx, Schumacher or some liberation theology before joining the call for an 'alternative development' which was in the interests of the poor and their environment rather than the interests of first world economies. At the end of the 1960s, Oxfam was nearly split in two by a group who thought Britain's leading NGO should withdraw from relief and development work to reinvent itself purely as a development education agency campaigning to make people aware of the injustices of current economic development.[6] In the end, it was agreed that the agency could do both. But, as in many British NGOs, a tension remained between relief and development objectives and priorities. Between 1980 and 2000, these tensions were resolved in three main ways: first by creating new organisations; secondly, by operational compromise and new notions of good practice, and thirdly by a conceptual shift from needs to rights.

One of the most entrepreneurial of Oxfam founders was a Christian businessman called Cecil Jackson-Cole. After helping to found Oxfam, he realised the need for other long-term development organisations meeting particular needs. His organisation, World In Need, functioned as something of a venture capital company for the British voluntary sector—and still does. It seed funded several new NGOs with particular development missions, including ActionAid and Help Age International. ActionAid was intended to fill the gap for an agency to focus wholly on children and long-term development without the in-house distractions of emergencies. Help the Aged was designed to meet the needs of a consistently overlooked group of poor people who were regularly missed out in development programmes. Such development-only organisations dealt with some of the multi-mandate tensions in the 1970s and 1980s. Ironically, however, in the 1990s both these development-only organisations found themselves setting up emergency units.

Another in-house way to solve the multi-mandate tension was to compromise operationally on the ground in a new concept of good practice that combined the best of relief and development orthodoxies. This good practice merger recognised that all good humanitarian work should be developmental, people-centred and capacity-build for the future while all good development work should always be ready for disaster. In short, emergency units in British NGOs had to accept the idea of more 'developmental relief' while their development colleagues had to swallow a commitment to 'disaster preparedness' and the rapid arrival of relief teams on their turf if an emergency occurred. This trade-off began in earnest in the early 1980s and continues to dominate British notions of best practice today.[7]

In the 1990s, this compromise was made all the easier when British NGOs discovered human rights and the so-called rights-based approach offered a conceptual way of merging the two fields. Many of the bigger NGOs reframed their missions and mandates in human rights terms so that poverty could be talked about as violations of civil, political, economic and social rights, and so too could disaster and war. The idea that 'we are all human rights workers now' helped ease the tension between humanitarian and development departments. These three developments have sustained a pragmatic British accommodation between relief and development goals and programmes over the years but they have never quite done away with a sense of two cultures: the impetuous cowboy relief worker who prioritises aid and action on one hand and the careful, touchy-feely development type who values solidarity and participation on the other. The best British agency staff have always done both fluently but usually preferred one or other role.

The Arrival of Managerialism

Just as British NGOs were beginning to come to terms with the tensions of their multi-mandates in the 1980s, they experienced a decade of massive growth. For example, when I joined SCF in 1983, its annual income was around 16 million pounds. By 1992 this had risen to 100 million pounds for the first time. All the big NGOs experienced growth of similar proportions because of increased government funding, more professional fundraising and the emergence of a new central political space for NGOs in world politics. NGOs' new political celebrity put them at the cutting and very visible edge of several world issues like famine, debt, the environment and also saw them mobilising the new phenomenon of the global advocacy movement to address such problems.

At the same time, however, this growth and higher profile gave them significant management challenges. Like their corporate cousins, large British NGOs were becoming complex trans-national bureaucracies. Their determination to develop global family associations like Oxfam International or the Save the Children Alliance compounded the managerial challenge. In response they looked to the commercial sector for management models to help them make these transitions.

At the end of the 1980s, the concept of strategic planning and strategic management arrived in many large NGOs. It has continued to dominate and transform British NGO culture to the present day.[8] In the last fifteen years, the senior managements of these NGOs have honed in on a range of key strategic objectives for their organisations and required that all parts of the organisation conform to these by planning and reporting to them.

The shift to strategic management has been a complex conceptual and cultural task and seen many years of what seemed to many like interminable re-structuring. The dreaded 'Logframe' came to symbolise this new managerialist organisation. Advocacy and programming were integrated in an effort to show results that could be scaled-up national and internationally and prove an NGO's strategic impact across the globe. To support this new approach, human resources departments were increasingly professionalised and recruitment given new rigour. In this process, country operations have tended to lose their autonomy to newly powerful regional management structures which have been located away from Britain in regional centres around the world and a new breed of NGO manager has emerged who oversees programme planning and reporting systems and rolls out new initiatives across the organisation instead of simply administering projects.[9]

Accountability and Legitimacy

It is not clear if or how the pendulum may swing back from managerialism but it is obvious that several British NGOs are now large transnational bureaucracies despite a continuing rhetoric that proclaims them to be innovative, fast-moving and reactive. From being Davids, several have come to look more like Goliaths. This new giant status in international politics has meant facing a new problem from the 1990s onwards—a very real political challenge to their legitimacy.[10]

Many politicians, journalists and citizens feel that the larger NGOs are punching far beyond their weight with agencies like Oxfam, Christian Aid, SCF and Amnesty able to exert extraordinary and quite asymmetric pressure on government and corporations alike. This has created a significant backlash summed up in a leading article in *The Economist* in 2002 which asked outright: 'Who Elected Oxfam?' British NGOs are in the process of responding to the legitimacy challenge by pointing to the broad base of their support, trying to prove their impact in more concrete terms, justifying their expertise and being more publicly transparent in their financial reporting and their learning as organisations.[11]

Rediscovering Humanitarianism

The 1990s were also highly significant for British NGOs as it saw them rediscovering the principles and practice of formal, classical humanitarian action. The lack of a Cold War dynamic to civil wars in the 1990s meant that, like all other agencies, British NGOs found themselves able to drive right into the middle of armed conflicts with the freedom and liability of being able to work between all sides in places like Bosnia, Somalia, Liberia and Afghanistan. Suddenly having to justify themselves and their presence to all sides, they rediscovered humanitarian principles and looked to the Geneva tradition of humanitarian action for inspiration and cover.

Overnight, traditional British words 'relief' and 'emergency' fell from the British NGO lexicon and were replaced by the word 'humanitarian' which had not been used routinely at all in Britain—except by the Red Cross—until the 1990s. In all the big British NGOs, emergencies departments became humanitarian departments, relief workers became humanitarians and their job titles changed accordingly. Like their cousins in the USA, British NGO policy staff and British academics began reading Jean Pictet, the Geneva Conventions and the Red Cross principles and adopting an ideological posture more akin to the Red Cross and MSF.

British NGOs began to espouse principle as much as pragmatism in the business of aid in war saying (passionately, of course) that their agencies were humanitarian, impartial and independent. Their long history of advocacy gave them a bit of a problem with being neutral, particularly as so many of them had been active in the solidarity-based humanitarianism of Central America's wars. Nevertheless, several leading British NGO figures and agencies were involved in producing the Code of Conduct, Sphere and the Humanitarian Charter, which sought to formalise humanitarian ideology and practice internationally. Really quite quickly, British NGO thinking began to orbit as much around Geneva as it did around its long history of charitable activism and its colonial tradition.

The next few years will tell whether British NGOs are able to continue being as Swiss and as French in their concern for principles and humanitarianism or whether they revert to a less ideological approach to helping people in war. Their history of multi-mandates, their instinct for state-building and the increasing influence of Islamic charity in the UK may see the pendulum of British humanitarian work swing back towards a more integrated and less dogmatic form of help. This may well take the form of a more activist concern for people's protection that focuses more on rallying political action and working across the relief-development-human rights spectrum.

British NGO Culture

The founders of Save the Children, Oxfam, Christian Aid and many other British NGOs were people from the heart of different parts of the British political, academic, religious or commercial establishment. They were entrepreneurs and radicals but ones who lived as part of the system and who represented an important constituency within it. To this day, most British NGOs, continue to use this insider-outsider position to great effect in a political system which remains at ease with the practice of respectably vocal critics. Opposition is still cherished in British politics and regarded as a difference of opinion rather than a radical confrontation. The long tradition of mainstream British NGOs—from anti-slavery to trade justice—sees politics as about winning an argument rather than mounting a barricade.

4

FRENCH OR ANGLO-SAXON

A DIFFERENT ETHICAL PERSPECTIVE?

Egbert Sondorp

That there is a difference between a French and an Anglo-Saxon approach is difficult to deny. But is it more than a caricature? Is there a real difference in the way issues are addressed, resulting in different action? And if this is the case, can this difference be explained?

In this chapter we will use the case of MSF to explore the issue of the French and Anglo-Saxon difference. MSF is clearly an organisation with strong French roots. But its ideas proved to appeal to a much broader group of people, literally around the globe. These days MSF is widely present in the Anglo-Saxon world. But it is still 'French thinking' that usually sparks off new debates within MSF to adjust to new challenges. It is as if the underlying paradigms do not seem to come naturally to the Anglo-Saxons. It will be argued in this chapter that a different ethical perspective may not fully explain the difference between the French and Anglo-Saxon approach, but may help in understanding it.

In describing some of the developments in MSF let me start with a personal experience. MSF France has existed since 1971, but only started to grow at the end of the '70s. This also led to the establishment of sections in other countries, including Belgium in 1981 and Holland in 1984. Initial relations between these autonomous sections were not that friendly and communication was kept to a minimum. To overcome this animosity, unwanted by many in the sections, some meetings were arranged between the more technical departments of the three sections to break the ice. So, as medical director of MSF Holland I met in Brussels with my French and Belgian colleagues. To my surprise the meeting was in French, a language I could hardly speak, and it was only thanks to my Belgian colleague who whispered some translation in my ear that I could follow the gist of what was discussed. Only later on did I discover that all participants in that meeting were perfectly able to speak English, but somehow it was not done those days to use that language.

Much has changed since then. It has often been the French, in Europe in general, but also within MSF, who have spearheaded internationalisation. And these days international MSF meetings can be expected to be primarily conducted in English.

Differences within MSF

All MSF sections are firmly rooted in the initial ideas as formulated at the time MSF France was established, the very home of the 'French doctors'. They all subscribe to the same Charter. But between sections there are differences. Those differences can largely be explained by the peculiar history of the various sections in interaction with their home environment. The case of MSF Holland in this sense is illustrative. The Netherlands, certainly in the days MSF Holland was established, used to be pretty much oriented to the Anglo-Saxon world. And, until today, that made a difference when comparing MSF Holland with some of the other sections. It is reflected in how issues are being debated, how decisions are being reached and how a lot of other management issues are being dealt with. In addition, the focus on purely humanitarian work, based on the overriding humanitarian principles of humanity and impartiality, was new in the Netherlands. Rather there was a strong tradition of medical work in developing countries as well as strong support for development aid, the latter in common with the United Kingdom and most Nordic countries. Pure humanitarian work, 'emergency aid', was looked down upon and MSF was just seen as a bunch of cowboys entering crisis situations to do their thing and leaving again before 'the real thing', i.e. development, could start. Why give a person a fish when one could teach him how to fish, was the archetypical question often asked. And this was reflected in the portfolio of project activities in the early days of MSF Holland, with much more emphasis on longer term projects, many with a developmental focus. But increasingly it was felt that this developmental approach was difficult to combine with pure humanitarian work. And after a hefty debate it was explicitly decided to close or handover the developmental projects and put much more focus on humanitarian action. Another lively debate within MSF Holland was around *témoignage*, witnessing, or as it is usually called these days 'advocacy'. This was in line with what the French founding fathers of MSF had in mind, to be able to speak out more easily than the Red Cross when confronted with gross human rights violations. Again, it took time before this stance was adopted within MSF Holland, where advocacy is now firmly ingrained in daily operations as part and parcel of the overall MSF activities. A third issue MSF Holland lived through in adapting to 'the French approach' was around the notion of 'independence'. How does independence to address the needs of people, another humanitarian core principle, relate to accepting funds from governments? For two reasons, the Dutch did not see too much difficulty in receiving funds from their own and other governments. This may partly be explained by operating in an environment where it is normal to receive development aid from governments. Another explanation may be that the Dutch, in common with most northern European countries and Canada, seem to have more basic trust in their governments and that humanitarian aid given by these governments does not necessarily come with political strings attached. And, therefore, independence was thought to be achievable by sufficient diversification of government donor agencies rather than not accepting government money. And while today one MSF section will be keener to minimise government contributions than another section, there is consensus that all sections should have at least a 50 per cent contribution from the public to finance their operations.

MSF Holland, from its marginal beginning with its cowboy image, grew into a well established, respected mainstream organisation, with widespread public support. Others have copied some of its relief work, but what remains is its unique focus on humanitarian work. It wants to address the needs of people trapped in conflict or medical crises, but does not aim to address root causes of conflict or to do peace building or to contribute to development.

Differences between MSF and Others

MSF is firmly rooted in the humanitarian tradition as articulated by Red Cross founder Henry Dunant and others, and proved to be a viable branch to this humanitarian tree. People in other countries were attracted to the ideas and started to import them. But here they had to compete with other prevailing ideas how to deal with poor and oppressed people. In particular in the Anglo-Saxon countries MSF has to compete with a number of much older, very well established NGOs. Secular agencies active in the humanitarian field such as CARE and IRC in the USA, and Oxfam and SCF in the UK, date back to the first and second World Wars. Today, these agencies together with a limited number of faith-based organisations, like World Vision and Caritas, and MSF have grown into multi-national families of NGOs with a presence around the globe. All are active in the humanitarian field, but—with the notable exception of MSF—all have given themselves a wider mandate. While MSF limits itself to the health sector and to a humanitarian relief context, the other large NGOs are all 'multi-mandated', with activities in different sectors operating in humanitarian relief as well as transitional post-conflict reconstruction and development work.

In its humanitarian work, MSF has a strong medical identity, primarily embedded in a curative tradition. Frequently arguments have come up to include other, related activities, like provision of food and clean water or large-scale distribution of drugs. However, time and again the notion of direct patient care prevails within MSF. The root causes of the kind of ill-health that MSF usually encounters can be sought in underlying poverty and/or conflict. Hence, both from within and from outside the organisation, many have argued that MSF should also address these root causes. But development or peace-building activities that would focus on these causes have very different dynamics. They are by definition political in nature and pose conditions, using carrot-and-stick methods to induce desirable change. However, this may conflict with provision of humanitarian relief based on needs alone. The key humanitarian principles of humanity, impartiality, neutrality and independence may be easily compromised. This is why MSF sticks to humanitarian relief. Many other agencies however, differ in opinion and feel that they can combine humanitarian relief and more development oriented activities within one, multi-mandate organisation.

Reverting back to an emergency approach in an area where development activities have started proves difficult, a fact that strengthens the MSF argument. Recent events in Darfur provide an example. Some of the major UK NGOs were present in the area prior to the current conflict, involved in development activities. When the recent conflict emerged they had great difficulty in changing their approach and were late to react. Or, as an MSF person remarked, 'it seems these agencies are only capable to send out policy analysts instead of relief workers'.

Humanitarian Versus Development

Why is it that an organisation like MSF, with its clear French roots, sticks to a more pure humanitarian approach, while most other, mainly Anglo-Saxon, agencies try to combine humanitarian relief with developmental activities? It is not because the approach of MSF is more comfortable. Its focus on pure relief may bring some glamour and work in the hot-spots of the world. But in most cases humanitarian work comes with lots of frustration, caused by prolonged confrontation with causal factors that cannot be addressed. Relief work in such situations is often described as reaching only the tip of the iceberg.

Two factors may not so much explain, but at least make it easier to understand why an organisation like MSF is so rooted in its approach. First of all, medical ethics are at the heart of the organisation. For doctors, at least for those trained in modern medicine's curative tradition, it comes quite naturally to focus fully on the individual patient and do whatever is possible to find a cure or to relief suffering. Usually those doctors will not look at non-biological root causes that may be the cause of their patient's illness nor will they look primarily at the cost of treatment. This attitude is very compatible with the humanitarian imperative, an important driver in humanitarian work. Other professionals seem to have more difficulty with this approach, making them more 'vulnerable' to include other activities like development. This would include those (clinical) doctors who have done public health training, which usually comes with a change in mind-set.

The second factor is related to different ethical perspectives people may have. In particular a difference between a primarily 'justice' ethic and a 'utilitarian' ethic. It may be this different *a priori* perspective that may be at the heart of a difference between a French and Anglo-Saxon approach. In a 'justice' ethic all people are equal and every individual should therefore have the same access to what they need as anyone else. The utilitarian ethic would want to pursue 'the greatest good for the greatest number of people'. I was once given a classroom example to explain the difference. According to the scenario, one has 100 pills and 100 patients with a disease that will kill them. Fifty of those patients need one pill to be cured, the other fifty need two pills. To whom would you give the pills? Usually three opinions emerge. A utilitarian argument would follow that by giving one pill to all patients who need one pill to get cured plus two pills to half of the patients who need two pills will cure the largest number of patients, i.e. seventy-five patients. Others will argue that all patients should have an equal chance to get cured, so should be selected at random. This comes down to curing sixty-six patients: thirty-three who need one pill, and thirty-three who need two pills. Yet others, confronted with this dilemma, want to avoid a direct choice, but would rather argue that more pills have to be found or that others, e.g. the community leaders, should decide who should be treated. There is no right or wrong, both ethical principles are perfectly defendable, but the example does show the practical consequences a choice may have.

A New Divide?

The case of MSF was used to try to understand some of the divide between a French and an Anglo-Saxon approach. The key difference seems strict adherence by MSF to a pure focus on humanitarian relief refraining from development or peace-building work.

But we are seeing rapid changes in geo-politics in the last few decades, with the end of the Cold War, the emergence and possibly current decline in many intra-state complex emergencies, the rise in terrorism and consequently new types of war. All this has important bearing on the humanitarian community. What may have divided agencies in the past may no longer be that important and new divisions may start showing.

Humanity, impartiality, neutrality and independence remain the leading humanitarian principles, subscribed to by virtually all humanitarian agencies. It was disagreement over impartiality that made the MSF Founders break away from the Red Cross, as the Red Cross was perceived to give more respect to state sovereignty than the obvious needs of people in Biafra. These days MSF and ICRC would be seen by most, both inside and outside the two organisations, as pretty close, and particularly different from other players. Both agencies' interpretation of neutrality is possibly the unifying factor. Development and poverty reduction means choosing sides and can therefore not be neutral, making up for a potential divide between the pure humanitarian agencies and other, multi-mandate agencies.

The war in Iraq highlighted a possible other difference between humanitarian NGOs, this time around 'independence'. This divide seems to be more between European and USA-based NGOs. US NGOs were seen by others to (be forced to) line up with the US government and its foreign policy objectives by being contracted to do the humanitarian work in and after the war against Saddam Hussein's regime. This divide highlighted a long-existing difference between US and most European NGOs. The latter would include both the more French as well as Anglo-Saxon agencies like the Red Cross, MSF, SCF and Oxfam. Despite their differences as described above they also have a common root in 'Dunantist humanitarianism', which aims to be disconnected from direct state interests. The US humanitarian NGOs have been labelled 'Wilsonian', after President Woodrow Wilson, where both US government activities and humanitarian action by NGOs are seen as serving the same good purpose.

Humanitarian work is under heavy pressure these days. It seems ever more difficult to address people's needs, where there is ever more vicious conflicts. Humanitarian space seems to diminish and humanitarian workers may become targets in the conflict. The 'death of humanitarianism' has been predicted after the 'humanitarian war' in Kosovo. A more hopeful thought is that the humanitarian idea is as alive as it always has been. An ever-changing world demands that the way the humanitarian idea is being expressed needs to be adjusted. Almost every major war causes adjustments to be made to the humanitarian system. The new era that the world has entered, in particular with the war in Iraq, is too underdeveloped to accurately predict what this will mean to the humanitarian idea and the way it is expressed. Consequences may be profound. Divides may be different from where they are now. This may even apply to the old French-Anglo-Saxon divide!

PART 2

SHOULD HUMANITARIAN ACTION
BE EVALUATED?

However much history—particularly when it is distant—is likely to bring together old enemies; the issue of evaluating humanitarian action, on the other hand, immediately whets the appetite to pick a fight. The basic question is as simple as it is explosive: is it possible or desirable to evaluate the action taken by NGOs to help suffering people? A simple question indeed when it is viewed in terms of action, expected benefits and the correlation between these two in order to measure impact. It becomes explosive, however, when it addresses an action which, in itself, is based on the principle of generosity, the simplicity of its means and the selflessness of its objectives. And if one brings into the equation the needs of local populations, the requirements of institutional donors and the expectations of private donors, one ends up with a question that has for a long time torn apart the humanitarian community. François Grünewald and Hugh Goyder provide an overview of the key issues whilst at the same time defining the terms of a dying debate, which is nevertheless still current.

5

EVALUATION FOR CHANGE

HOW CAN WE IMPROVE THE IMPACT OF HUMANITARIAN ACTION?

François Grünewald

Until recently, statements such as 'what we do cannot be assessed' were often heard in the humanitarian world, perhaps giving the impression that humanitarians were afraid of evaluations and criticism from outside. The policies of funders, who often confused audits and impact assessments, did not help, nor did the links between programme evaluation and individual performance assessments. Considerable progress has been made: the role of evaluation is finally beginning to be recognised and 'quality' processes are the order of the day.

The quality of action and the different definitions that refer to it are now at the centre of the great humanitarian debates, as shown by the often vigorous, even passionate, written and oral discussions seen at the end of the 1990s and start of the 2000s[1] on approaches such as the Sphere Project. The subject is definitely worthwhile. From the jungles of Eastern Congo to the deserts of Darfur, from the snows of Afghanistan to the mangrove swamps of Sierra Leone, from the ruins of Iraq to those of Haiti, come too many testimonies of unsuitable aid, poor-quality programmes and wasted money. But we also get news about creative innovations, efforts made and progress achieved. In the last

51

few years, humanitarian actors have been rolling up their sleeves and working to 'do better'.

However, significant differences of approach have emerged. The challenges are such that the debate has changed into a confrontation between Latin approaches to humanitarian practice and action and other more British approaches, and with this a risk of deadlock. The specific quality tool-building approach, such as the one used for the development of the Quality COMPAS—a quality management tool based on the concept of quality assurance—provides an alternative way of resolving this dispute, even though it continues to be systematically ignored by British NGOs. Its central objective is to ensure the quality of actions undertaken to help vulnerable populations and to defend the independence of humanitarian actors engaged in helping them.

Numerous initiatives have been set up, sometimes with significant financial resources, and attempt to co-ordinate themselves within a framework of exchange known as the Quality and Accountability Initiative. Similarly the launch of a system of clusters by the United Nations since 2006 helped part of the situation to evolve. However, the debate remains complex due to the diversity of approaches.

Quality: At the Heart of New Challenges

In industry, quality is measured by the ability to provide customers with the maximum level of satisfaction (or the optimum, depending on the desires of targeted customers). The search for quality has given rise to national and international standards and certification systems. Historically, quality processes only emerged because 'powerful' customers needed to be satisfied. They were powerful because they could go to the competition when quality was too low. The degree of dissatisfaction or the economic significance of rejection determines the sanction. Goods that do not satisfy are taken off the shelf and out of the production chain. The quality issue that concerns humanitarian organisations is our capacity to satisfy the needs of people who are not customers in the strict sense, but populations in distress. These 'strange customers' have not usually chosen to become victims, refugees or displaced persons. Since their situation is often dramatic and the balance of power between them and humanitarian actors unequal, they have little choice: lack of quality and unsuitable solutions are, therefore, rarely punished.

When they are, this can sometimes take the form of serious security incidents caused by frustrated and/or humiliated people. In the humanitarian world the word 'quality' was, for a long time, uncommon. It took a long time for initiatives like Sphere, Active Learning Network for Accountability and Performance in Humanitarian Action (ALNAP) and others to incorporate the concept, preferring instead 'compliance to standard' to 'quality project responding to the needs of the population', as if the two concepts were equivalent to each other.

A study of the humanitarian sector carried out by quality and management specialists within Groupe Urgence-Réhabilitation-Développement (URD) led to the following four simple conclusions:

1. In a troubled environment, quality is necessarily the result of efforts made during the whole exercise: in the humanitarian sector, it concerns all the different phases of the project cycle. It is managed proactively, based on the knowledge of the critical points where errors and other non-quality factors appear and which must be managed as you go along.[2] This approach is similar to quality assurance.

No real improvement in the quality of interventions is possible without 'client' involvement (beneficiaries, victims, partners, call them what you will) in the process. In the humanitarian sector, this could mean the need for participatory approaches to action design. Between 2000 and 2004 Groupe URD conducted a research project on this theme—The Global Study on Consultation and Participation of Affected Populations in Humanitarian Action—and in 2009 issued a trilingual (French, English and Spanish) manual on the aims and methods of engaging with local populations.[3]

2. There can be no quality dynamic without a learning procedure, including the establishment of regular *ex-post* evaluations of programme processes and impact; and notably not without a systematic reflection on the management of negative effects brought about by aid. The quality of humanitarian action cannot be measured according to compliance with procedures or technical standards, but by an approach to impact, even if that is extremely complex: 'Did it make a difference?' To quote the former Head of Humanitarian Affairs at the UK's DFID, Dr Mukesh Kapila:

> In a displaced persons camp, an NGO built a water distribution system based on reservoirs and a large number of supply taps dotted about the camp. All technical standards were complied with, including water quality. But what the women wanted was a single water point, slightly isolated,

which could have become this place of social exchange and intimacy reserved for women they needed so much to rebuild the relations destroyed by displacement and camp life.

3. Quality therefore requires a learning/evaluation process, the repetition of experiences that are assessed every time. However, one can only evaluate action or assess the impact of different factors (stakeholder activities, stakeholder/target population interaction, external factors) by developing from the outset a coherent monitoring and evaluation process of that action. With that objective in mind, the Quality COMPAS set out to give the same frame of reference to the whole project cycle, from diagnosis via monitoring to the evaluation of actions.

4. Quality is never a given. It is the result of real professionalism which must be demonstrable, constant ethical vigilance and a process of democratic and transparent institutional management (governance). As mentioned above, the quality of programmes is the result of patient repetition, during which lessons are learnt. Hence the need for evaluations that yield advice and are aimed at change, learning and improvement. To ensure the effectiveness of humanitarian action, the proposed approach is one of accountability to the victims as well as to those millions of unknown people whose taxes and gifts enable us to work, but also to our teams on the ground and the civil societies of countries affected by crises.

For almost two decades funders have wanted to be reassured about how their funds are used. After all, they are also accountable to their constituents and electors and have audits and financial controls for this purpose. They are sensitive to administrative optimisation efforts of the ISO 9000 kind.[4] But, increasingly, they want to know that the aid delivered has made a difference, and had an impact. They have therefore started conducting their own evaluations. NGOs felt as though they couldn't afford to miss the boat. So, in 1995 MSF Holland organised the first international conference on the evaluation of humanitarian action. European Community regulations have led the ECHO to increase the number of evaluations. Since then there has been an explosion of evaluations by and for funders, by and for the United Nations, by and for NGOs, to such an extent that we have sometimes reached saturation point. How many of these evaluations have led to lessons being learnt?[5] There are still many steps to take to make evaluation a real tool for institutional change, but some interesting directions are in the process of being tested: processes to monitor the implementation of recommendations; innovative practices in evaluation which move away from the classic process and introduce new models; Real Time Evaluation (RTE); After Action Review (AAR); self-evaluation; peer evaluation; iterative evaluations with feedback mechanisms, etc.

Is there a New French/Anglo-Saxon Conflict around Quality Issues in the Humanitarian Field?

The fear of seeing standardised, consumerist thinking, sometimes presented under the guise of rights-based approaches by the main Anglo-Saxon players, taking a decisive place in the humanitarian movement and potentially betraying its ideals, is not completely without foundation. Seeing Sphere manuals being used by the Russian army in Grozny and by the American army in Afghanistan and Iraq can only raise concerns and lead to a redefinition of the issues at stake.

The only way to do this is to revert to the humanitarian principles and not to mere technical questions. It is on these principles that the Projet Qualité was set up in 1998 and by returning to these fundamentals that the more recent Synergie Qualité approach was developed. Indeed, it seemed that the only effective way to simultaneously manage the ethical aspects, programme outputs, personnel policies and reporting to donors was to use a systemic approach.

But is this complex questioning the result of a conflict between the French and Anglo-Saxon approaches? It sometimes appears that way. In the legal methods that we have acquired from the US, there are elements that may have shifted the debate towards the kind of 'judicialisation' that so exasperates the French and Latin world. This worry is reinforced when Sphere was closely linked to the Ombudsman Project, or when a great number of documents related to the Humanitarian Accountability Project (HAP) mention the Sphere Standards as the reference to be followed, under penalty of sanctions. On the other hand, the Quality COMPAS draws from quality assurance principles developed in the US more than forty years ago. Evaluation, participation and accountability,[6] which are at the heart of Anglo-Saxon humanitarian culture, are questioned and often not understood by French NGOs. Nevertheless, these themes have formed the basis of the work and approach of Groupe URD since its establishment more than fifteen years ago. In fact, the nature of the differences that have come to light since 1998 during the course of these debates follow other lines of fracture than a simple opposition between the French-speaking and English-speaking world.

The first issue is that of differing dynamics and above all what differentiates civil society. Some approaches want to bring together local action and global thinking. This requires the development of coalitions and groups to promote ideas. Large humanitarian agencies involved for a long time in collective action require codes of conduct and adherence to projects such as Sphere or HAP to give them political weight. This category, which appears to aim at rallying everyone behind a single leader, is mostly composed of major British and American agencies. The ECB2 project which reunites the major British and American players is the most recent example of this.

Others advocate local action and global recognition, preferring strength in weakness, the disturbing clamour of the isolated troublemaker. The 'French doctor' movement, which for a long time has been neither French nor limited to doctors, works better with this approach and remains very sceptical of large, collective groups.

Another approach is to enhance the value of comparative advantages. One of the key elements of the French approach is to favour diversity and heterogeneity rather than size and cohesion. Although it can be dangerous, it is often the only way to manage highly complex and dynamic situations, where the diversity of actors and responses helps to overcome many obstacles. The monolithic nature of the Anglo-Saxon approach makes it more difficult to deal with the cracks and faults in the system. While Groupe URP published an article 'Working with Complexity and Turbulence—and Becoming Friends With It'[7] in 2003 this theme has only been taken up by Anglo-Saxon authors in 2008 (in an article by Peter Walker of Tuft University[8]).

The second issue concerns relations with the state and the question of independence. Some NGOs seek contact, synergy and alliances with the state, and are prepared to take the relationship quite far, including sub-contracting. For these NGOs, establishing regulated agreement mechanisms with the state is essential. More importance is therefore given to implementation criteria and technical standards than to ethical challenges and solidarity issues. However, as states also desire regulation mechanisms, this movement in the humanitarian community aims to take the lead and establish its own rules. This is Sphere's approach. The easy movement of staff between the army, the civil service and NGOs, which is common and accepted in America and Britain, raises

French humanitarians' hackles, even if some big names in the 'French doctor' community have themselves passed through the oak-panelled corridors of power.

For others, the freedom of each institution has to be preserved at all costs in relation to donors, other agencies and multiplying techniques and methodologies. Participation in collective action or outside their very focused family is out of the question. They reject large multi-actor coalitions through fear of losing their character, their specificity and their independence.

The last few years have shown that there are openings for dialogue and bridges to be built, but also that dividing lines remain, and will take time to cross. Is such diversity an impediment? Yes, if it leads to inefficiency and loss. Funders or some parts of the humanitarian community will then be tempted to reduce and regiment it. No, if it turns out to be a source of enrichment and the necessary capacity to occupy the niches which become more and more precious in the context of serious insecurity and the 'clash of civilisations'.

Having joined the debate surrounding the Sphere project, the Groupe URD team has seen it change. The new manual contains real improvements, but could have been even better if they had waited for the results of the Sphere evaluation. Indeed, the report underlines that the Humanitarian Charter, the strengths and dangers of which were pointed out above, must be revised. Can one advocate quality without applying to oneself the few fundamental principles, such as the need for evaluations in order to progress? This raises interesting questions regarding the accountability and strategy of the Sphere project, which French humanitarians have tried to answer through projects such as Synergie Qualité and the Quality COMPAS. Thus, is the newsletter 'Cap sur la qualité',[9] which regularly reports information about the difficulties and successes of users of the Quality COMPAS, a mechanism to support the permanent improvement of the tool (continuous quality improvement is at the heart of the approach of those concerned with quality).

For a 'Quality' Approach

Launched in 1998 as a breakaway from Sphere, the Qualité project launched a collective approach which is reflected in the context of Synergie Qualité. This recent initiative hinges on five principles: ethics, governance, human resources, diagnosis and evaluation, and satisfaction of target populations. The Quality COMPAS, a quality management operational tool developed by Groupe URD and integrated into Synergie Qualité, connects these issues in a two-fold strategy: providing a consistent and comprehensive tool ensuring that quality assurance is included in all project cycle phases; and developing reference criteria that are common to both the action management and the evaluation phases.

The approach of the quality compass is based on field work, not on the compilation of guidelines or the organisation of technical meetings, like Sphere but on the patient identification of critical points, during every mission and by carefully reading dozens of evaluation reports. From this, a quality reference base was developed, leading to the identification of twelve criteria, organised into a quality reference framework, the compass rose.

Integrating, refining and often going beyond the Development Assistance Committee (DAC) criteria, the articles of the Red Cross Code of Conduct and sometimes reinterpreting elements of Sphere, the quality compas aims to remain a non-prescriptive tool primarily based on questioning. This approach also applies to satisfaction: whose satisfaction? Recipients? Who are they? Satisfaction with regard to what? Needs, wishes, individuals? How can it be measured? From the start, the Plateforme Qualiti took a stand against those who wanted to establish complaints mechanisms: complaints about what? Non-compliance with Sphere standards? Malevolence? Acts that are punishable by law (prostitution, corruption, etc.) Or war crimes? To make humanitarians carry the can for aid that is often ill-adapted in a world where the causes of disasters are often in the hands of warring parties who rape, kill and torture, but also where donors make decisions that often dictate possible responses, seems inappropriate in relation to the real problems: should the humanitarian sector be the new area in our collective lives where recourse to the legal framework is necessary?

The work of Groupe URD in the context of the global study on participation by affected populations in humanitarian action between 2000 and 2004 underlined the importance of a partially forgotten paradigm: the strongest roots of satisfaction can be found in the involvement of populations in the humanitarian aid processes that concern them. In the field, this translates to satisfaction of need through more appropriate aid, satisfaction of men and women through being actors in their own future. Then again, there is a disjunction between the idea of participation and the assumption of knowing what is good for people, such as is implied in the text of spheres technical indicators.

The starting point of research on quality conducted by Groupe URD and its partners from Synergie Qualité[10] is absolute respect for the dignity of victims of crises. These actors, who have sometimes been present on the ground for more than thirty years, recognise the singularities of men and women encountered in crisis sites. It is through this paradigm of proximity, this exchange between two human beings, one who is suffering and the other who wants to help, that humanity, the fundamental principle of humanitarian action, is born. It is also by recognising their diversity that respectful relations arise. Each situation is different; each human group has its own rules, cultures and criteria. The notion of average victim is not only an aberration in operational terms (peoples food, water and shelter needs vary according to conditions, sex, age, culture), but it is first and foremost a denial of dignity. Doing ones best to meet the needs of each person, not in a standardised manner but in an adaptive way, is at the root of the principle of impartiality.

Our position is neither idealistic nor naive. The search for improved involvement of affected populations so as to make the voice of victims heard should not make us lose sight of the fact that, like any society, these beneficiaries are structured by social relationships of power, oppression and exploitation. Suffering people are not necessarily devoid of ulterior motives, nor are those who help them and claim to legislate aid. It might be considered politically incorrect to say so, yet in this search for dialogue, quite a few have been manipulated. The principle of independence arises from this ability to listen based on the in-depth analysis of contexts and power relations.

Human beings are not just bellies to fill, heads to shelter or mouths to water. They are all that and much more. To answer the cries for help of those from whom war, flash flooding or volcanic eruptions have taken everything is, first and foremost, to return to the principles of humanity, impartiality and independence. To do this well is to give ourselves the correct tools to understand, to listen, to monitor and implement our programmes; all are useful pointers to help learn from our mistakes and our successes. In short, real quality steps.

6

LEARNING, MONITORING AND EVALUATION

Hugh Goyder

Firstly, it is necessary to define 'monitoring' and 'evaluation'. Monitoring is the systematic and continuous collecting and analysing of information about the progress of a piece of work over time. Evaluation is an assessment at one point in time that concentrates specifically on whether the objectives of a piece of work have been achieved and what impact has been made.[1] Evaluation has now become an integral part of how the humanitarian sector operates. Evaluations were found to expose organisations, teams and individuals to critical appraisal and provided a means of assessing when, where and how problems were addressed. However, there was a lack of clarity as to whether the objective of evaluation was to provide a practical tool for supporting organisational learning or whether evaluation of humanitarian action (EHA) was merely intended to create greater upward accountability to donors. There was a tendency to attempt to combine the two objectives, which in many instances led to a lack of attention to issues of organisational learning.

Moreover, in 2001 the international organisation ALNAP commissioned a review of how agencies responded to the recommendations made by humanitarian evaluations.[2] The findings showed that recommendations were rarely linked to learning processes and that practical follow-up after evaluations—especially when evaluation was designed as a stand-alone activity—was poor. This of course is not unique to

61

EHA but is endemic in the evaluation field as a whole.[3] Too many evaluations are left to collect dust on agency shelves. The need to better integrate evaluation into overall project management cycles and internal policy debates could not have been clearer. This, in turn, required backing from senior management and integration of the planning of evaluation into ongoing management frameworks, such as monitoring.

The problem of evaluation utilisation was analysed in more depth by ALNAP in 2006. This valuable study not only raises fundamental questions about why humanitarian evaluations are not better used, but it also highlights the need for other tools to be used: this study concluded that 'the impact of evaluation is enhanced, if not enabled, by being part of a broader menu of approaches to enhancing performance. Monitoring, for example, remains a poor cousin of evaluation and has yet to receive the same attention from decision-makers. Evaluation, in whatever form, is only one element of accountability'.

Some worrying observations were made as to the limited impact that evaluation findings and recommendations were having on field practice itself; and this corroborated findings from the follow-up study. In other words, why invest so much in evaluation if lessons from past experiences are not being learned? In spite of some improvements in the quality of evaluations, there had been little impact on learning and a corresponding absence of any significant change in humanitarian action.

Constraints identified in the humanitarian sector included the following:

- Incentive structures in agencies that promote defensive behaviour and a culture of blame.
- Short-term funding mechanisms that militate against a learning environment for field staff.
- Very high rates of staff turnover within ongoing programmes and between programmes.
- Lack of clarity as to intervention objectives and desired outcomes.
- Training provision not properly linked to learning processes.
- Poorly developed mechanisms for learning between different organisations

This chapter reviews the constraints that impede agencies' abilities to learn and explores how different tools can be used to address these dysfunctions. Specifically, we will ask whether monitoring can become more than a data collection exercise and transform itself into a valuable vehicle for 'learning whilst doing'.

Monitoring and Learning in Real-Time

The experiences of the past few years both within the humanitarian sector and the wider evaluation field have thus contributed to a desire in ALNAP and the humanitarian community to look beyond evaluation to see how other approaches may contribute to learning. Partly as a consequence we are now seeing an increase in new kinds of activities such as real-time evaluations (RTE), strategic review and self-evaluation. These aim to make up for deficiencies in traditional *ex-post* evaluation and are intended to provide a timely, rapid review of a particular response so that findings can be used to feed into ongoing decision making processes.

The United Nations High Commissioner for Refugees started the trend, closely followed by the World Food Programme, ALNAP's learning support office (Malawi lso) and the HAP. The UK Disaster Emergency Committee (DEC) has also carried out some 'monitoring missions' that closely resemble RTE.

Alongside RTE, other 'real-time' monitoring practices have increasingly been acknowledged as potentially important, though often neglected. The renewed interest in these activities is motivated by the concern that *ex-post* evaluations often come too late to affect the operations they assess and, given the weak institutional memories in many organisations, too early to influence the next operation. *Ex-post* evaluations will in some cases support learning, in particular where there are mechanisms for the integration of evaluation findings. However, the structure of many agencies militates against such integration: in some UN and donor agencies, for example, evaluation offices are often kept separate from programming branches and report directly to the executive director's office—in order to ensure a greater independence of the evaluation function. This practice, though highly desirable in theory, can in practice make it harder to ensure that evaluation findings have a real influence on future programming work. One reason may be that organisations underestimate the time and effort it takes to follow up and implement the recommendations of an evaluation, even in those cases where the recommendations have been accepted.

Monitoring, on the other hand, is an ongoing agency function that is generally integrated into everyday programming. And as opposed to *ex-post* evaluation, monitoring may be able to offer a 'short action learning loop'.[4] The importance of this cannot be underestimated given that information from monitoring can potentially enable mid-course corrections of programmes. It could also provide information for humanitarian field workers and potentially empower them to make better judgements during the course of their immediate work. In this respect one area where monitoring has a distinct advantage is its potential to examine social process, such as why interventions are or are not working, who is benefiting, and why.

But monitoring will require more attention if this is going to happen. Conclusions from analysis of the 165 evaluation reports over the three years of the annual review strongly support the notion that the current quality of monitoring is poor. Can monitoring 'fill the gap' by playing a crucial role in both broad sectoral learning and in helping field workers make critical judgements in the midst of humanitarian crises?

Learning and Downward Accountability: Is Monitoring a Missing Link?

While evaluation remains an important tool for upward accountability—to donors, headquarters and auditors—it is clear that there are still prevailing learning and downward accountability gaps, the latter especially to the primary stakeholders. Edwards and Hulme comment that accountability is generally interpreted as 'the means by which...organisations report (upwards) to a recognised authority... and are held responsible for their actions, with insufficient attention directed "downwards" to the views of the intended beneficiaries'.[5] Yet downward accountability has both a practical and an ethical dimension. Practically, improved downward accountability will support closer consultation and participation of affected people in the design and implementation of interventions. This means interventions are more likely to reflect genuine needs and priorities, and achieve optimum impact. Ethically, downward accountability is embedded in the values and principles central to humanitarian action, notably the Red Cross/ Crescent Code of Conduct and the humanitarian charter, and in recent years efforts to improve this kind of accountability in the humanitarian sector have been led by the Geneva-based humanitarian accountability project. Thus a commitment to downward accountability is part of the living value system that should underpin all humanitarian action.

Initial findings from the ALNAP-commissioned global study on the consultation with and participation by affected populations in humanitarian action, as well as the findings of the annual reviews, suggests that there is a dearth of good practice in involving the affected population in the delivery of humanitarian aid.[6] Similarly, findings from the three HAP field trials in Sierra Leone, Afghanistan and Cambodia describe the challenge in finding and institutionalising adequate methods of effectively listening and responding to the needs and concerns of affected populations during the course of humanitarian operations.[7]

One change in recent years is that there is now far greater awareness about the Red Cross/Crescent NGO Code of Conduct—which contains a commitment to downward accountability—which has now been in existence for nearly fifteen years. From 1997 onwards this Code of Conduct has been much re-enforced by the Sphere project which was launched by a group of humanitarian NGOs and the Red Cross and Red Crescent movement. According to its web site:

Sphere is based on two core beliefs: first, that all possible steps should be taken to alleviate human suffering arising out of calamity and conflict, and second, that those affected by disaster have a right to life with dignity and therefore a right to assistance. Sphere is three things: a handbook, a broad process of collaboration and an expression of commitment to quality and accountability. (www.sphereproject.org).

In spite of these international initiatives it is unclear whether all the good ideas and intentions about accountability to affected populations have as yet really resulted in changes in practice. As regards evaluation, the cumulative three year findings of the ALNAP's annual reviews up until 2003 suggest that 86 per cent of reports were rated as unsatisfactory in terms of consultation with, and participation of, primary stakeholders in the evaluation process. Despite some good practice, EHA still tends to give insufficient attention to the views and perspectives of primary stakeholders.

A fundamental issue in terms of changing mind-sets within 'traditional' humanitarian action relates to the extent to which those involved in monitoring, strategic review and rte are willing to enter into dialogue with primary stakeholders. Usually rushed evaluation exercises allow limited time for such dialogue, while ongoing monitoring over a period of several months offers the opportunity for longer term contact, with repeat visits to the same site, household or individual which should lead to both improved situation analysis and understanding of impact. One of the key differences between evaluation and monitoring, is that evaluations are normally done by external consultants who at the end 'take away' much of the learning. Monitoring is led by field staff and the lessons it generates can at least in theory, remain in the agency. But the quality of monitoring depends crucially not just on the quality and confidence of the staff themselves, but the extent to which they are encouraged or discouraged for pointing out and documenting problems in implementation as they arise. As argued above, high turnover of staff makes high quality monitoring less likely.

A key question is thus whether monitoring systems can be designed to support downward accountability given agency structures that are usually hierarchical. Normally information flows from the field to country offices and thence to HQ. This is not necessarily about replacing specific monitoring activities but rather about being clearer about what monitoring is intended to achieve and how, as well as changing mind-sets about what monitoring can and should accomplish. Currently, monitoring activities tend to be a repository for a wide assortment of implicit and explicit aims and objectives related to learning and accountability. When problems arise, there is a tendency to call for 'better monitoring', without analysing the nature and content of current monitoring and the resources required either to improve the quality of existing efforts or to take on additional tasks.

Greater downward accountability may mean that monitoring moves further in the direction of RTE and strategic review, as introduced earlier. Of course there are unanswered questions as to how RTE differs from strategic review, and how they both differ from monitoring. This will depend on how an agency defines the scope of monitoring itself. Since monitoring is usually associated with direct management tasks, especially data collection, the difference between these approaches may depend on how real-time evaluators and those involved in strategic review are able to take a step back from day-to-day reporting and administration and use their time for analysis, making sound judgements, and involving primary stakeholders.

An important issue raised by Sandison in her 2006 study on evaluation utilisation for ALNAP was the lack of trust between evaluators and the staff of the agencies commissioning the evaluations. As she argues, insufficient attention is paid to the relational side of evaluation, and the trust between evaluators and agency staff can break down all too easily. This is made more difficult by the fact that evaluators are brought in for only a short contract, and neither they nor their clients may give sufficient importance to building strong relationships. Even if there are good intentions on both sides, there may simply not be the time for this kind of trust to develop. This again suggests the need for tools other than evaluation to increase learning and accountability.

A System Under Strain?

Reviewing the wider picture of how monitoring fits into humanitarian agencies, one finds a system under great strain. Two key points can be identified. First, there is an increasing internal reporting burden on field staff and agencies due to multiple reporting demands, increasing earmarking from donors, and a proliferation of cross-cutting themes (for example, human rights, gender equality, environment, even humanitarian accountability itself), all of which are important but all of which bring their own reporting requirements. Anecdotal evidence suggests that multiple accountability initiatives are viewed with trepidation by field staff—not necessarily because they will reveal malpractice but because they could lead to a time-consuming round of additional workshops and reporting. In the end these initiatives may be more about repackaging field-level knowledge as 'quality assurance' information for donors and HQ rather be used in practical support for addressing some of the real dilemmas faced during implementation.

Second, there are significant problems in enhancing monitoring in relation to human resource practice, especially when taking into account the excessively long hours of work and high levels of staff turn-over, both of which mitigate against providing the time needed for staff to be able to contribute to, and learn from, the information produced by monitoring. The failure of good ideas about accountability and learning in order to generate and maintain widespread good practice may be indicative of the kind of pressurised work environments that humanitarian aid workers actually experience. It is within this context that genuine incentives—through monitoring and other means—must both be learned and applied. Instead of coming up with additional tasks there is a need to look at how people try to solve problems and make sense of their situation within prevailing duties and responsibilities. The overwhelming quantity of information and reports that many offices have to produce may reflect a lack of awareness of the actual pressures of fieldwork in terms of poor communication between field and HQ. But the concern is that increased information flows may be at the expense of efforts to help transform information into knowledge, especially the need to embed efforts in an awareness of the context in which affected people struggle to survive and the potential impact of aid on their very survival.

In this respect there seems little point in developing yet more methods and/or toolboxes if they are not preceded by a concomitant effort to streamline existing data collection responsibilities. While information needs will vary according to different organisational cultures, the contexts in which monitoring is happening and the balance each agency requires between reporting for upward and downward accountability, there seem to be only a few positive signs. There is, for instance, an emerging awareness among donors and operational agencies that harmonisation of reporting requirements is needed to free up resources for other tasks. This must be a first step. Learning can only be improved if field staff are given the time to do it. The key message is one of sector reform.

Linking Relief, Rehabilitation and Development (LRRD)

Improvements in monitoring for both learning and downward accountability depend to a large degree on the expectations as to what humanitarian assistance sets out to achieve in the first place. Humanitarian programming today, for example, whether in Sudan, Afghanistan, or the Democratic Republic of Congo is increasingly intermingled with rehabilitation. Humanitarian assistance is no longer only about saving lives but must also relate to the root causes of conflict and poverty. The sector is being called upon to deliver aid in a way that can ultimately reduce violence and promote recovery, development and peace. This ambitious agenda has major consequences for learning, downward accountability and performance. If these aims are genuinely to be realised, monitoring needs to become more than just a vehicle for upward accountability and must be redirected towards providing contextual information to fill gaps that currently exist between the relief, rehabilitation and development phases of response.

A significant proportion of humanitarian funding is actually being spent on activities normally associated with rehabilitation, development and evaluators are increasingly paying attention to this shift. Yet while the sector is beginning to ask the right questions as to LRRD, there are major deficiencies in finding the right answer there is a short-term success in most direct emergency interventions, especially in health, water and sanitation, and food aid, but we constantly need to review the extent to which these short term successes result in any real lasting benefit. For example, clean water is provided in camps but in longer-term maintenance is carried out by community groups. However, spare parts for pumps are lacking so that water cannot be provided on a more sustainable basis. Furthermore, there is still too little capacity building of government and local institutions, especially local NGOs and community-based organisations in improved humanitarian responses. Too often the most vulnerable are more likely to slip back into destitution when the initial phase of the relief intervention is over. Many humanitarian evaluations have to be conducted very soon after an emergency intervention has been completed, as the donor wants to close the project file, and these longer-term impacts of relief work are rarely captured in most evaluations.

Perhaps the basic issue is whether it is realistic to expect-longer term and more sustainable impacts from emergency interventions? LRRD policies paired with short funding cycles and often unrealistic completion targets have created pressure on agencies to make unrealistic claims about the prospects for recovery in order to 'declare victory' and move on to the next humanitarian crisis. The move to results-based management in the sector has supported this tendency towards results inflation. In reality, the most vulnerable are being left behind as the rhetoric of LRRD moves ahead. When struggling to rebuild their livelihoods, the destitute, the disabled and the landless often lack the resources to keep up with the project cycle. And, at the same time, agencies tend to ignore the coping strategies and capacity of affected populations.

The failure of LRRD on the ground is mirrored by the failure to find a useful synergy between the relief and development communities. Development actors who have knowledge about the nature of ongoing vulnerability and risk are still not engaging with the humanitarian agencies that 'parachute in' when, for example, structural food insecurity turns into acute famine. Recent experience in southern Africa has taught us that chronic vulnerabilities caused by HIV/Aids and changing political economies mean that the boundaries that are supposed to separate relief and development are becoming fainter still. Understanding the nature of chronic risk is something that needs to be addressed in various ways—by researching, reviewing and changing both practice and policy.

We would argue that all these issues relate to a continued failure, within the humanitarian sector, to look more closely at the wider impacts of the aid provided on the lives of beneficiaries. Downward accountability means more than caring about whether the food was delivered and the bellies filled. It means caring about livelihoods too. Humanitarians may only have relatively blunt tools at their disposal with which to ensure that people are not hungry tomorrow, but that does not absolve the sector from the need to sit with development actors to discuss what needs to be done. And monitoring has an important role to play in providing information and feedback at key moments in the LRRD process.

PART 3

NGOS ON THE NEW GEOPOLITICAL CHESSBOARD

'Embedded', the expression used to describe journalists accompanying coalition troops engaged in the first Gulf War, epitomises the vulnerable position of NGOs in a changing world. For the 'second' Iraq War, the US army unilaterally decided to allow into the country only those NGOs that accepted its conditions. Some accepted, others refused, but it was impossible to make a distinction between 'good' and 'bad' NGOs. That would have been too simple: the dividing line between humanitarian ethics and assistance to victims is not always clear. Does the ambiguity maintained between military and humanitarian action, between the M-16 and the stethoscope, hide a broader agenda? Sami Makki and James Darcy report on the twenty-first century humanitarian sector.

7

INTERNATIONAL NGOS UNDER FIRE

CAUGHT BETWEEN THE GLOBAL FIGHT AGAINST TERRORISM AND NEO-LIBERAL APPROACHES TO SECURITY GOVERNANCE

Sami Makki

The proliferation of emergency crises since the end of the Cold War led to the increasingly frequent deployment of civil and military actors to deal with complex situations. Since then, co-operation between actors on the ground and at political and strategic level has been considered necessary. Following the failure of the Somalia intervention in 1993 and the co-ordination problems encountered during Operation Uphold Democracy in Haiti in 1994, the US government created an institutional system to enhance the consistency of multi-dimensional responses to crises.

Since 9/11, the war against terrorism has transformed the conditions of Western interventions. According to American strategic thinking, failed states, which are considered as potential shelters for radical Islamic terrorist networks, constitute a threat. Based on this assumption, a real change in civil–military relations can be observed in the United States. More broadly, Western states, under the auspices of the United States, are reclaiming the initiative in humanitarian action, which is being integrated into other components of diplomatic and military action. Given the strength of the US political and military machinery and its influence on the strategic policies of America's allies, the challenges arising from the militarisation of civil actors cannot be ignored by Europe. They need to be assessed in order to measure all their implications for future multinational interventions in conflicts where the privatisation of violence is expanding.

Military and Humanitarian Action: A Dangerous Mix

Failure to observe the neutrality, impartiality and independence of the humanitarian space has led to an increasing lack of security for humanitarian personnel. This trend is not entirely new: between January 1992 and September 1998, 153 humanitarian workers lost their lives. However, things have been worse since 9/11. On 28 July 2004, following the assassination of five of its voluntary workers in a premeditated attack in north-west Afghanistan, MSF announced the closure of all its programmes and its retreat from the country after twenty-four years.

Increasing insecurity has affected employees of the United Nations agencies, the International Committee of the Red Cross (ICRC) and NGOs. On 19 August 2003, twenty-seven UN staff were killed and 426 people were injured by a bomb in Baghdad. On 27 October 2003, the ICRC headquarters were hit, while on 22 July 2003 an ICRC employee was assassinated. More than thirty humanitarian workers, mostly Afghans, have been killed in Afghanistan since the beginning of 2003. Because of the confusion between military forces and humanitarian workers, denounced on several occasions by humanitarians, aid is no longer perceived as an impartial activity, a fact which endangers the life of voluntary workers and reduces access to populations in distress. Furthermore, the impunity afforded those responsible for the attacks is proof that the Afghan authorities are not carrying out their responsibilities for protecting humanitarian workers on their territory. Faced with this rapid degradation in the safety of humanitarian workers, a resolution was adopted by the Security Council in August 2003, calling for the protection of all humanitarian personnel; unfortunately it had no real impact on the practices of warring parties. Worse, coalition forces have shown themselves to be unable to guarantee the safety of civilian personnel. For the last five years, whilst systems of instrumentalisation of humanitarianism have developed, there has been an increasing lack of security for aid workers. Researchers from the Overseas Development Institute (ODI) found that, 'in 2008, 260 humanitarian aid workers were killed, kidnapped or seriously injured in violent attacks. This toll is the highest of the twelve years that our study has tracked these incidents'.[1] Thus, contrary to what certain studies have claimed, it seems now clear there is a link between the two phenomena, notably when these attacks are carried out for political reasons in places where the international presence is considered sensitive (Darfur, Somalia, Iraq and Afghanistan).

In Afghanistan, members of the American Special Forces and PRTs, small security teams composed of civil and military staff responsible for reconstruction activities, have regularly used humanitarian symbols without ensuring the protection of humanitarian staff, even though the PRTs are in charge of security. To the American officer in charge of the coalition's civil–military co-ordination centre, the significant technical work carried out by PRTs, including the number of rebuilt buildings and infrastructure, shows that NGOs and coalition forces have exactly the same objectives. With this kind of logic, an independent and neutral humanitarian space is no longer conceivable.

In dealing with complex humanitarian operations, multinational interoperability aims to expand the scope of operations from military jointness to civil-military integration by including non-governmental organisations and private military/security companies. With the increased insecurity on the ground, as described above, the use of deterrence strategies for security management of civilian actors is slowly becoming a norm with new standards among Allies under US leadership. Although already developed in non-governmental networks, this privatising trend comes from changing government practices.

The Marketing and Privatisation of Humanitarian Aid: A Prelude to New Conflicts?

By choosing to outsource international aid policies to implement the 'privatisation of aid' announced by President Bush in 2002, the US government accelerated the emergence of the commercial sector as an intermediary in relations between the US federal government and NGOs, in a drive to improve the government's financial health. The increasingly greater emphasis placed on commercial organisations has gradually changed traditional criteria and the nature of NGOs' relations with other actors in conflict. Gradually, a number of American

NGOs have shifted from advanced co-operation to contractual partnership with USAID, further reinforcing the relations of interdependence and forcing all three sectors to formulate and develop concerted strategies. Surviving associations often dramatically change their management style, taking inspiration from the commercial sector.[2]

Private Security Companies: Out to Conquer Humanitarian Markets

The marketing approach to humanitarian action through public–private partnerships has led to the emergence of private companies providing logistical support or security services. Under pressure from donors concerned with cost-effectiveness, the nature of American and British humanitarian action is becoming technical, focusing on logistics (food distribution, refugee camp construction), and neglecting basic humanitarian principles and a true acknowledgment of the 'acceptance strategy' as a possibly efficient management of security. Events in Iraq show clearly that private actors are present during essential conflict and post-conflict phases and that they fulfil functions that are indispensable to the exercise of force by the United States. They are its cornerstone. In 2003, with 20,000 private security personnel present in Iraq, or the equivalent of 15 per cent of total Western armed forces—a 'healthy situation', according to a high-ranking coalition official interviewed in Paris in May 2004—the privatisation of peace operations is no longer an option, but a gradual process of 'pushing back the limits' of outsourcing of functions traditionally carried out by armed forces and the state.[3] In 2008, according to the American expert P.W. Singer, more than 180,000 private operators occupied military functions, previously managed by coalition troops. The announced retreat of US forces will not ease this problem. With the same amount of private military operators in Afghanistan at the end of 2009, US and British generals officially recognised, in recent London and Paris conferences in early 2010, that the process had gone too far and it was a worrying trend for the future Western armies and operations.

Hybrid Actors Eliminating Identity Barriers to the Detriment of NGOs

For several years now, large numbers of private companies have been lobbying and using propaganda to present themselves as reliable and expert partners in the management of peace operations, even as 'new humanitarian agencies'.[4] The services they offer range from passive protection (of UN agencies or NGO convoys) to assisting armed forces (demobilisation, disarmament and the reintegration of combatants). Their client list is vast, including the US, British, Swedish, Canadian and Swiss governments, UN agencies, the European Commission, the ICRC and large international NGOs.[5] The latter also contribute to the development of these new private companies, whilst in the Middle East, several thousand former military officers are employed under security contracts by United Nations and humanitarian agencies.[6]

The American Model of Civil-Military Integration: Still Influential in Spite of Repeated Failures

In the context of the global fight against terrorism, new approaches to change in US foreign policy take on a crucial dimension. As early as October 2001, then Secretary of State Colin Powell was stating that American aid agencies constituted 'force multipliers': they were the 'agents of American foreign policy' and the 'instruments of war' against terrorism. Large American NGOs, factors of power and drivers of American influence, constitute an essential pillar of a global strategy based on the development of information networks. These powerful trends have led to resistance, creating a 'growing cultural rift between NGOs and the American government' at the end of George W. Bush's first term in office.

The Synchronisation of Humanitarian Activities for Strategic Purposes

US doctrine on interagency co-operation states that advanced co-ordination forges a vital link between the military and civilian instruments of power as well as non-state agencies and that 'obtaining co-ordinated and integrated effort in an interagency operation is critical to success'.[7] The integration of NGOs into operations started with the institutionalisation, from 1997 onwards, of the US 'interagency co-ordination' process between the State Department, the Pentagon and USAID, through the integration of civil–military systems to manage humanitarian crisis. Under the cover of a streamlining process (to avoid duplication of civil and military systems) to ensure a continuum between the stages of emergency, re-establishment of peace, reconstruction and development, USAID fills gaps in US human information and strategic influencing systems.

Due to the need for operational efficiency (planning, command unit, real time necessity) and the lack of civil initiatives, control was originally left to the military. In addition to institutional factors, constant interaction between non-governmental civil sectors, business, universities/experts and members of government and military agencies facilitated the emergence of common values, a common language and a common culture in civil–military operations. Within the large NGOs or USAID, former officers often hold key positions in planning and liaising with the armed forces or security management—an important factor in the propagation of military culture. The integration of civilian personnel and systems by the armed forces has been adapted to the war on terror. The American model of civil–military integration aims to transform the battlefield in favour of the armed forces. By developing asymmetrical approaches, the Pentagon is a catalyst of both emergency and the imposition of a military operational tempo on civilian actors. This militarisation of humanitarian space and time is intended to enable the US armed forces to conduct network wars or 'netwars' to win hearts and minds of civilians in counter-insurgency operations.

The Iraq war highlighted the essential role played by USAID's Disaster Assistance Response Teams (DARTs), civilian teams specialised in emergency assistance, and the Pentagon's Civil Affairs Experts. Interconnection between all levels of the civil responsibility chain has been developed through the DARTs. Although creating operational frustrations and institutional discontent, these actions exemplify the militarisation of the humanitarian sector as a result of a balance of power favouring defence at political and strategic levels in order to control the interagency process. As analysed by Robert Egnell, the armed intervention Iraq is a significant example of a 'divided approach to civil-military relations' leading to the failure in Iraq. When the Department of Defense is given the full responsibility to lead the process of post-conflict planning without properly, including the expertise and resources from other departments and agencies, this can easily generate militarised solutions.

In order to ensure greater civilian oversight, the Office of the Coordinator for Reconstruction and Stabilisation was set up, in the summer of 2004, within the US State Department. The mission of this Office, managed by an ambassador officially appointed in October

2004, is to 'lead, co-ordinate and institutionalise US government civilian capacity to prevent or prepare for post-conflict situations, and to help stabilise and reconstruct societies in transition from conflict or civil strife so they can reach a sustainable path toward peace, democracy and a market economy'. Originally, the Office was staffed by thirty representatives of the State Department, USAID, the Department of Defense, the Central Intelligence Agency (CIA), the Army Corps of Engineers, Joint Forces Command and the Department of the Treasury. The US government also plans to deploy a specialised Humanitarian, Stabilization and Reconstruction Team (HSRT) to combatant commands, to participate in post-conflict planning where US military forces are engaged. This just goes to show that the civil control of these interventions will not be further guaranteed by such a structure, especially if the civil budgets are not considerably strengthened. US armed forces usually resist strongly any attempts to implement change, with a preference for big conventional war, 'mobilising maximum force used to win swiftly and decisively [...] with a US military cultural emphasis on casualty avoidance and a reliance on the "silver bullet" of technology'.[8] Although very dynamic, the US interagency system is 'caught in the political system of checks and balances, in which distrust and competition are central'.[9]

Continuity and Change in the US Interagency Efforts

The DoD's Quadrennial Defense Review (QDR) of 2006 acknowledged the importance of irregular warfare and the need to adapt civilian and military capabilities to ensure greater integration. Beyond the elements of continuity, President Obama initiated key reforms to the benefits of the civilian sector. In early 2010, a draft version of the Presidential Study Directive (PSD-7): A New Way Forward on Global Development was leaked to the media. The paper, developed by the National Security Council (NSC), illustrates the Obama administration willing to take a major step forward on improving U.S. global development policy and involving non-state actors in the process.

Although very supportive of the initiative, InterAction issued a statement in early 2010 to express its regrets concerning the lack of 'serious dialogue among the Administration, Congress and civil society on how best' to implement the report since '[this report] could be a major step toward establishing international development as a core pillar of

U.S. foreign policy'.[10] This would have been an interesting opportunity to improve the level of trust between humanitarian NGOs and military representatives weakened by a series of controversial agreements signed under high budgetary and funding pressure to overcome resistance.[11]

To ensure greater balance in civil-military relations, the State Department's Civilian Response Corps established in 2008, as well as the Center for Complex Operations (CCO), created in 2009 under the Center for Technology and National Security Policy (CTNSP),[12] are key institutional innovations in charge of facilitating and implementing change both at the national and multinational levels.[13] At a transatlantic level, according to Cassidy, a careful examination of British and American Peace Support Operations Doctrines indicates that doctrines for armed humanitarian operations diverge, reflecting significant differences in military strategic cultures (i.e. beliefs, attitudes and values). In spite of this existing 'diametrically polar approaches to force [...], US and British doctrine writers have conducted a series of meetings during the writing process to exchange ideas and co-ordinate, with the aim of creating 'compatible doctrine' since the mid-90's.[14] In the name of interoperability, mutual efforts were produced to codify new 'gray-area' operations, tactics, techniques and procedures, aimed at limiting the influence of national cultural preferences and differences in terms of civil-military relations. Although very contentious, this operational experiment of the concept of 'synchronised, joint and integrated operations' explains the central role of the 'comprehensive approach' in the new NATO Strategic Concept of 2010.

Military Traditions, Interoperability and Risks of Strategic Acculturation: British Experience, French Reforms

A British study published in 2003 stressed that 'interoperability among the military forces of North American and European Nations is a matter of concern' for integrated multinational missions. NATO defines interoperability as 'the ability of systems, units or forces to provide services to and accept services from other systems, units or forces and to use these services so exchanged to enable them to operate effectively together' with a specific aim at 'enhancing operational effectiveness and improving efficiency in the use of available resources'.[15] Although expressing the need to ensure interoperability in technological and military terms, this definition suggests a strong link between interoperable systems and efficient use of resources, notably in an era of credit crunch and changing security environment, justifying a 'forced consensus' on strategic matters[16]. Lessons learned and continuous search for best practice in complex peace operations are key drivers to achieve unity of command and effort.

Within the European Union, the British, drawing on the lessons of intervention in Sierra Leone and Iraq, have made the civil-military question into an important politico-strategic stake. The inter-agency co-ordination on security is the result of numerous reforms encouraged from above by the implementation of 'Joined up Government' passionately desired by Tony Blair. From the involvement of British forces in preventative missions, through 'Defence Diplomacy' to 'Conflict Prevention Pools', reforms have been effectively led.

During the twentieth century, the British Army remained engaged in imperial policing, with constabulary missions, counterinsurgency operations and small wars, reinforcing the links between the Foreign Affairs and the Ministry of Defence. The military had to adapt its format and culture to complex civil-military operations imperatives when necessary, without relying on technology as a panacea or substitute for troops on the ground.

According to Egnell, the British failure in Iraq could be explained by Britain's inability to operate according to the traditional way of war. Acting as a junior partner within a multinational coalition under US leadership, Britain was not responsible for strategy and had a limited influence over the US approach. This difficult position was reinforced by a weak strategic direction by Prime Minister Blair who favoured secrecy and isolation rather than openness and transparency. The search for cost-effectiveness through greater interoperability within the coalition led to a marginalisation of alternative military cultures and civil-military patterns which were better suited for stabilisation and reconstruction operations. In the 90's, the Conflict Prevention Pool aims to improve the efficiency of the United Kingdom's contribution to conflict management by integrating strategies (Ministry of Defence-DFID-Foreign and Commonwealth Office)—'when an integrated approach brings added value'—through cross-subsidised Security Sector Reform programmes in Africa (Sierra Leone, Kenya, the Great Lakes region, Burundi). Wider civil–military co-operation takes place through a strong partnership between DFID and large British NGOs, as well as British NGO networks and coalitions acting at national or international level, such as British Overseas NGOs for Development (BOND) or the European Peace building Liaison Office (EPLO). Despite similarities with the American approach and the political will of the British government to extend the integrated approach to stabilisation operations with a new Post-Conflict Reconstruction Unit, the British context allowed NGOs to limit government ambitions, at least to some extent.

The United Kingdom has a tradition of cross-government co-operation, a more centralised parliamentary political system able to exercise control over the military. Also, the expertise mobilised to tackle international security challenges comes from all relevant ministries and agencies allowing a permanent dialogue and 'reconciliation between policy and militaries matters at all levels from joint civil-military advice to the leadership'. Therefore, professional civil servants can create 'trust at the institutional as well as the interpersonal level' and it 'emphasises flexibility, minimum use of force and civil-military co-operation—which are all considered essentials for effective conduct of complex peace operations'.[17]

In France, the doctrine of 2005 defined civil-military co-operation as:

the operational function destined to improve the integration of the military into its human environment in order to facilitate the accomplishment of its mission, the re-establishment of a normal state of security and the management of the crisis by the civil authorities (administrative, humanitarian, economic recovery)... The support given to civil protagonists must never compromise the fulfilment of the mission. The activities that it leads will be transferred to civil bodies as soon as possible.[18]

Amongst the reforms announced in the White Paper on defence and national security of June 2008 was the emphasis placed on 'the importance of civil and mixed civil-military operations in the management of crises'. It announced the development of new capacities for the Ministry of Foreign Affairs, notably by the setting up of an operational oversight centre and support for the management of external crises, ensuring competence for the preparation, monitoring and exit from international crises. In looking for 'the synergy between the military and civil components of interventions', the French civil-military operation inexorably moves closer to the integrated model, inspired by the US at the transatlantic level.

NATO's Comprehensive Approach: Bridging the Doctrinal Gap between Allies

2010 has been a crucial year for NATO transformation with renewed efforts to create a positive environment for the production of a new strategic concept. In the context of a global counterinsurgency campaign, with a challenging mission in Afghanistan, 'NATO has taken the first steps toward developing the Comprehensive Approach initiative that would enable the collaborative engagement of all requisite civilian and military elements of international power to end hostilities, restore order, commence reconstruction, and begin to address a conflict's root causes'.[19] Following a Danish initiative of 2005 and the Riga Summit of 2007, an international initiative was launched under the direction of the CTNSP at the National Defense University in Washington to further develop operational research on post-conflict stabilisation and reconstruction operations.

European Resistance or Uncertainties Surrounding the Integrated 'Multifunctional Strategy' of the European Union

Recent developments in the European Security and Defence Policy (ESDP) present a real challenge for future humanitarian policy in the European Union. The ESDP is based on the principle of a 'global and coherent crisis prevention and management capacity' that includes both the military and civilian crisis management capacity to lead so-called Petersberg Missions (humanitarian missions aimed at peacekeeping or the evacuation of nationals). With the increase in the number of actors deployed, there is a risk of adding to the confusion and therefore to the insecurity of humanitarian workers. The draft Constitutional Treaty contains provisions affecting ECHO's humanitarian policy,[20] and although the mention of 'neutral' and 'impartial' humanitarian interventions in the EU's external action provides some guarantees, uncertainties remain as to the preservation of the civilian nature of humanitarian aid.

After the first phases of experimentation, notably in African theatres of operation, one must ask what was the role and the objectives of the civil-military planning cell put in place under the auspices of the major states of the EU? While spaces for dialogue and co-operation between the European bodies involved in the implementation of the security strategy have multiplied over the last three years, can we speak of a definitive resolution of the rivalries between intergovernmental institutions (Headquarters, Military Committee, Political and Security Committee (COPS) defining and implementing the ESDP) and EU institutions (Directorate General for Development [DG DEV] and ECHO) that are in charge of humanitarian aid and development management? In accordance with the security strategy of the European Union (the Solana report: 'A Secure Europe in a Better World' adopted by the European Council in December 2003 and its Implementation report of December 2008), these operations aim to prepare a multifunctional and coherent capacity of the whole military, diplomatic, commercial, industrial or humanitarian instruments the EU has access to, for a strategy of integrated action. Many humanitarian NGOs, special partners of ECHO, fear the risks of politicising humanitarian action to the detriment of the principle of neutrality above all, which governs humanitarian action. While the European Consensus on Humanitarian Aid of December 2007 hoped to protect humanitarian actors who were now the politics of development—defined in the broadest sense which could extend to certain humanitarian activities to an institutional point of view—who must be integrated into the security politics of the EU. In the December 2008 'Report on the Implementation of the European Security Strategy—Providing Security in a Changing World', the link between security and development was strengthened. Numerous elements suggested that the Swedish presidency would make this problem the central point of its action in favour of the ESDP, notably through the reform of the security sector. The Lisbon Treaty's entry into force, at the end of 2009, was the final green light for the implementation of European integrated systems and solutions to complex crisis situations.

The strong influence of this integrationist current is also visible across the implementation of very specific systems of reform of the UN humanitarian system. If the search for advanced co-ordination, for greater efficiency in the assistance given to victims, can be judged acceptable by some humanitarian actors, there are numerous criticisms concerning extreme integration of structures.[21] Seeing the situation of their British and American counterparts, their concern is understandable.

The Limits of Integration: A Process Doomed to Failure
in the Short and Long Term

Although sought-after, integration poses numerous risks. By seeking to establish an integrated, holistic and complex system, the military establishment is creating an interdependence between civil and military approaches to conflict and post-conflict management. The current phase of the stabilisation operation in Iraq highlights the limits of a strategy whereby military failures endanger assistance programmes to the civilian population. Although activist NGOs have criticised the Bush administration, large organisations have preferred to distance themselves from the troubled masses so as not to risk displeasing Republican leaders, due to their financial dependence on the federal government. In the lessons learnt from the Iraq intervention, the United States does not seem to see the political dimension of this failure, preferring once more to focus its approach on technological dimensions. It views this regional crisis from a global perspective, which reinforces a complete separation of global and local temporalities.

Finally, by seeking to gradually privatise humanitarian crisis management and peace operations, the dominant approach, which is much quicker to apply practices based on New Public Management, seems to easily confuse the effective management of its own system of intervention according to its own criteria (number of fatalities in the armed forces, political consensus, return on investment) with real help for affected countries (rather than that which is simply proclaimed, as is the case in Iraq and Afghanistan), to enable them to reconstruct themselves.

The American and British civil–military integration strategies, as they are currently being implemented through the reconfiguration of security and development nexus, aims to give an increasing role to commercial actors, including those offering technical support services, and even conducting certain military operations. These private actors often operate in informal networks (public–private, political–industrial, mercenary–paramilitary–security) that favour the elimination of the bureaucratic processes of political control and evaluation, including corruption and criminality, and lead to the weakening of developing states.

Despite the specific nature of the civil–military debate in the United States and the United Kingdom, focused on a strategic consensus between government and non-government actors, it would be wrong to underestimate the scope of dissenting voices from civil society, of alternative analyses by research centres and criticism by some NGOs. Given the international challenges resulting from the new security agenda, a projection of future humanitarian developments should highlight the limitations of American and British governmental approaches and maintain that alternative approaches are possible. Practitioners, theoreticians and researchers should work together to redefine the key to a common identity more respectful of international law and peoples.

8

PATRONAGE OR INFLUENCE?

INTERNATIONAL POLITICS AND THE CHANGING ROLE OF NON-GOVERNMENTAL HUMANITARIAN ORGANISATIONS

James Darcy

Dramatic changes in the international political landscape in recent years have exposed fundamentally differing conceptions among international non-governmental organisations (INGOs) about their proper role in relation to political power. This is evident not least in attitudes to the use of military force on humanitarian grounds, which some are increasingly willing to support, even to call for, while others see it as contrary to the very idea of humanitarianism. It is evident, too, in differing attitudes to the donor-agency relationship, to the new global security agenda, and to the role of INGOs in post-conflict state-building projects. From a range of perspectives, the major international aid agencies have both helped shape the political landscape and are now more than ever significant 'players' in it, both individually and collectively. Yet their influence is felt in very different ways. From highly adversarial positions involving public denunciation of governmental policies, to close engagement with government policy formulation and implementation, INGOs have cast themselves in very different—and sometimes mutually incompatible—roles in relation to political authorities. This is true both in relation to international donor governments and the governments of crisis-affected countries. The following pages briefly explore a number of linked themes, each of which reflects different aspects of this diversity of INGO approaches.

Divergent Approaches

The question of how INGOs should relate to political power is perhaps the most contentious of the various issues on which these agencies are divided. A divide exists between some of the European agency families and others, particularly those originating in the US; a divide sometimes crudely (and inaccurately) framed as a divergence between Francophone and Anglophone agencies. In fact, the debate is far from being simply bi-partisan: major differences of view exist within these 'camps'.

An apparent divergence exists between the approaches of two different kinds of agencies. The first consists of the more specialised humanitarian agencies whose archetype is the ICRC, and whose primary organisational focus is on emergency medical, food and public health agendas together with the protection of civilians in war zones. For these the approach to political power has been to maintain strict independence of action, if not neutrality of position. Some in this group—though not those in the Red Cross and Red Crescent Movement—have adopted an instinctively adversarial approach to political power. The second group consists of the multi-mandate (humanitarian/development) agencies that have tended to embrace the wider, more ambitious agenda of the 'new humanitarianism'. For these, collaborative engagement with political authorities has tended to be a more comfortable mode of operation, particularly as donor government policy (and hence also host government policy) has increasingly adopted the language of pro-poor development and of avowed concern with humanitarian principles. This remains true in spite of the widespread adoption by these agencies (and some donors) of human rights approaches, which despite their revolutionary origins have lost much of their adversarial characteristics in the consensual post-Cold War era. Finally, the nature of the development project itself and a concern with addressing structural causes encourages agencies in this second category to play a long game, in which the adversarial approach may be perceived as counter-productive.

The nature of agencies' mandates and their operational agendas cannot of itself explain the divergence of approaches. The origins of these agencies, and the national political and cultural contexts in which they have developed, lie at the heart of this divergence. Abby Stoddard has charted the distinct origins and evolutionary path of 'Wilsonian' agencies in the US, which see humanitarian and US foreign policy goals as essentially complementary; and contrasted this with the 'Dunantist' agencies which tend to stress their independence from (and often opposition to) government policy.[1] A clear divide between faith-based and secular agencies is hard to delineate, at least as regards their public positions. But rhetoric is only part of the issue: the inclination to collaborate with or maintain strict independence from political authorities is perhaps a more telling indicator. Here some trends are apparent. In the US, in particular, a marked trend towards government implementation of humanitarian programmes through faith-based INGOs has been apparent since advent of the Bush administration in 2001.[2] This appears to reflect both a move away from multilateral towards bilateral modes of engagement in crisis situations, and also a distinct preference concerning the nature of the implementing partner for aid programming.

The cases of Afghanistan and Iraq, in which the US Government has played diverse roles as aggressor, occupying power, security provider and lead donor, have exposed more sharply than ever the divergence of agency approaches—and the ambivalence of those who would instinctively collaborate on reconstruction and development agendas but who fear identification with the occupying power and its interests. This fear extends to the very real risk that such identification may pose to the safety of agencies' local and international staff. Some agencies—MSF, Oxfam—refused to take funding from the UK or US governments to work in Iraq. Others took money for reconstruction but not relief. The crisis of identity among humanitarian agencies has been felt most acutely in the post-Cold War era where their major government sponsors have themselves been directly involved as belligerents. But these issues are not limited to interventions in war zones. In North Korea, for example, the apparent convergence of political and humanitarian agendas has resulted in a massive programme of food aid and other forms of relief, provided largely through US INGOs and delivered on terms that stretch the principles of impartiality and independence up to (and arguably beyond) the limit.

Sharply divergent opinion can exist within international agency families. So, for example, a headline dispute between Save the Children

UK and Save the Children US in 2003 revealed very different views on the appropriate stance in relation to the parties to the war in Iraq. An article in the Guardian newspaper on 28 November 2003, headlined 'How British charity was silenced on Iraq', reported that:

One of Britain's most high-profile charities was ordered to end criticism of military action in Iraq by its powerful US wing to avoid jeopardising financial support from Washington and corporate donors, a Guardian investigation has discovered. Internal emails reveal how Save the Children UK came under enormous pressure after it accused coalition forces of breaching the Geneva convention [sic] by blocking humanitarian aid.

Leaving aside the accuracy of the report and the extent to which it is representative of agency practice, it appears to demonstrate very different attitudes on each side of the Atlantic, related in large part to a concern (on the US side) not to adopt a position that ran directly counter to the strongly-held views of its major donors and supporters.

A Faustian Pact? INGOS and the Quest for Influence

The divergent evolution of agencies' roles has not been accidental, even if it has not always been the result of deliberate strategic choice. Those who have pursued the path of closer proximity to power and closer engagement with international policy-making are perhaps more consciously motivated by a desire for 'strategic' influence, premised on constructive engagement and collaboration. The symptoms of this include the burgeoning of INGO liaison offices in key policy centres like New York and Washington, Geneva and Brussels. But engagement with political processes is one thing; alignment with government policies is another. Since the events of 9/11 in particular, a significant proportion of (predominantly US) INGOs have seen their programmes become more than ever an avowed part of the foreign policy of their respective donor governments. In a speech to NGO heads in 2001, the US Secretary of State Colin Powell famously expressed the idea of NGOs as 'force multipliers'. Two years later, the Administrator of USAID, Andrew Natsios, took a similar line in a speech to US INGOs at an InterAction Forum in 2003, stating the proposition in startlingly frank terms. Natsios insisted that aid agencies and for-profit contractors in the field should identify themselves as recipients of U.S. funding to show a stronger link to American foreign policy. If this does not happen more often, Natsios threatened to personally tear up their contracts and find new partners. NGOs and contractors 'are an arm of the U.S. government', Natsios said.[3]

In his earlier speech, Powell had (perhaps paradoxically) made a point of stressing the importance of NGO independence, saying 'it is the very fact of your being independent and not an arm of government that makes you so valuable, that permits you to do your essential work…'. Natsios evidently did not agree, and adopts a line that stresses the contractual over the partnership nature of the relationship. There is nothing particularly new in this: it can be seen as consistent with the 'Wilsonian' approach described above, albeit with new emphasis on the principal-agent hierarchy. But this was a much more overt and extreme formulation of that doctrine and it caused considerable debate and dissension amongst US agencies. As Stoddard describes[4] 'Despite the traditionally pragmatic character of many US NGOs, and their willingness to find ways to work with political and military actors when the situation demands, the largest and most reputable are not prepared to be seen as direct agents of the US government'.

Clearly there are market factors as well as ideological factors at work here, though these are sometimes hard to disentangle. Agencies have always tended to follow the money and official money goes where it is politically expedient to spend it.[5] From another perspective, the changing international power structure and security agenda have led to the emergence of new kinds of government-INGO relationship, and a marked intolerance from the New Right in the US for dissenting NGO voices (witness the establishment of 'NGO Watch' in 2003 to monitor the activities of left-leaning INGOs). The US NGOs are seen by the US Government as essential partners in the war on terror. Michael Ignatieff[6] portrays this role as part of the civilizing mission of a new imperial project, analogous to the former role of missionaries. Funding these agencies enables the invader to demonstrate compassion, to win hearts and minds. Colin Powell, addressing the NGOs, used the language of values: 'Your very presence in these places, your diversity, your dedication to serving humankind sends a powerful message about America and our value system to people all over the world…' Such an appeal to a common identity and purpose across the governmental-NGO divide would be almost unthinkable for most Europeans.

The dangers inherent in this proximity to power have been variously articulated.[7] Perhaps they can best be summarised as the danger of co-option or 'instrumentalisation': the loss of capacity for independent action by humanitarian agencies, and the subordination of humanitarian to political agendas. Recent debates about UN integrated missions and their effect on 'humanitarian space' in contexts of violent insecurity have centred on this and related staff security questions. Critics of those who adopt a politically collaborative role point to the dangers this poses not just to the particular agency, but to others by association. When humanitarians become associated with political/military agendas, it is argued, the space for truly humanitarian (impartial, neutral, independent) action contracts. Some—notably in the MSF family—go further, and construct their humanitarian identity precisely around the idea of opposition to power.[8] As Jean-Hervé Bradol puts it 'Opposed to power but not actively engaged in its conquest...humanitarian action is necessarily subversive, since partisans of the established order rarely empathise with those whose elimination they tolerate or decree...' While this arguably transposes one form of political engagement for another, it represents a very different conception of the proper role of humanitarian actors vis-à-vis political actors from those outlined above.

So have the 'collaborators' sold their souls in their quest for influence? Most importantly, have they jeopardised or compromised the humanitarian agenda,[9] or have they helped to bring it to the centre of the political agenda? Some would look for absolute answers to this question; others would say that it can only be considered case by case. The key measure must be actual outcomes, understood not in terms of the achievement of wider political goals (including peace) but in the strictly humanitarian terms of life saved and suffering alleviated in the shorter term. Arthur Dewey of the Bureau for Population, Refugees and Migration in the US State Department mounts a robust defence of the humanitarian benefits of effective collaboration between political, military and humanitarian actors.[10] He highlights in particular the necessity of this collaboration in pursuit of the protection aspects of the humanitarian agenda. In a similar vein, Ignatieff[11] argues that humanitarian action is in many cases contingent upon the willingness to intervene with force. What is surely true is that the scope for humanitarian action in any given context may, in practice, depend upon the extent to which reasonably safe access has been secured by military force. This in turn exemplifies a more general truth: that humanitarian outcomes (good or bad) will generally depend on political action as much as—or more than—they depend on the actions of humanitarian agencies.

If political engagement is generally acknowledged to be essential to the humanitarian enterprise, what forms of engagement are dangerous? Does working with an integrated UN mission, for example, and accepting its scheme of priorities in a given context amount to co-option and the subordination of the humanitarian agenda? Some would say so and point to cases like Angola to support their argument.[12] A dangerous form of 'group think' is said by some to characterise such situations, where the desire to pursue multiple agendas leads inevitably to compromises which can be fatal. The case for the defence is not so clearly or so passionately articulated, perhaps because the agencies concerned feel no particular need to do so—the collaborative approach for some is unarguably preferable to the alternative. Yet the dilemmas are real, even if they can be overstated and over-simplified. At what point does negotiation with a political actor, or engagement in a political process, tip over into collusion, compromise and wilful neglect? The UN is sometimes argued to represent a political 'firewall' for the INGOs, playing the diplomatic front role that allows INGOs to operate in the political cracks and avoid becoming bound into compromising roles. But some of the larger NGOs, in their maturity, have become rather too bulky and inflexible to be able to slip easily through the cracks any more. There are those who feel that the increasingly indistinguishable roles and positions of UN and INGOs signifies a net loss of capacity for independent humanitarian action.

Policy Coherence and the Pursuit of Multiple Objectives

The multi-mandate agencies—those who pursue humanitarian and development goals in tandem—face some particular issues in their approach to complex emergencies. The logic of development, at the heart of which is the enlightenment notion of a perfectible (or at least progressively improvable) world, sits uncomfortably with the humanitarian's fundamentally pessimistic world view. Humanitarians are prophets of doom; and like Cassandra, they may be right, but few (especially developmentalists) may wish to hear the message. Most importantly, the humanitarian imperative is uncompromising in its demands: it claims priority over all other calls for the advancement of public goods. The 'relief-development continuum', now largely abandoned as a model, served in part as a way of reconciling the competing claims and approaches of the relief and development agendas, at least at the level of management.[13] But as 'post-conflict' transitional contexts like Afghanistan demonstrate, this approach does not in fact resolve strategic or programming dilemmas. Assumptions about complementarity of agendas tend not to survive translation into practice; and there remains an unresolved tension between 'substitutory' and 'capacity-building' approaches in contexts where state capacity is weak or absent. There is a widely felt need for alternative models here.

When other policy agendas like peace and security are added to the mix, the tensions become still more pronounced and a choice may be faced between fundamentally incompatible strategies. As the example of Darfur illustrates, pursuing a quest for peace may require a choice as to whether, and how, one could pursue a humanitarian or human rights agenda, in cases where the parties to the conflict (and the peace process) are themselves pursuing war strategies that involve attacking civilians.

Part of the issue the multi-mandate agencies face is that the 'problem', as presented, is so multi-faceted and the 'solutions' apparently so interdependent. Poverty and human suffering, civilian protection and peace-building, are all of comparable importance, are causally related, and the solutions to them (or at least the appropriate responses to them) apparently interconnected—just as the corresponding rights agendas are, since the Vienna Conference of 1993, deemed to be 'indivisible and interconnected'. But as Rieff[14] points out 'the definition of tragedy... is the conflict between two rights and, if anything becomes clear through the increasing complexity of humanitarian engagement, it is that not all good objectives can be reconciled'. In theory, the humanitarian imperative provides a basis on which to establish priorities; but the broader the interpretation of the humanitarian problem, the less useful this proves as a normative device.

The pursuit by donor governments of cross-departmental policy coherence has resulted in some strange hybrids. As Duffield & Macrae put it[15] 'In their promotion of an integrated approach to peace, it is assumed that the objectives of aid, diplomacy, military and trade policies are necessarily compatible'. In practice they have not always proved so. The danger here is not just that highlighted by the multi-donor evaluation of the Rwanda crisis response (1996) that humanitarian action is taken as a substitute for effective political action. As Macrae[16] writes '...humanitarian organisations ... need to be aware that rather than being simply a substitute for political action, they might be becoming the primary form of political action undertaken by the West'. She warns of threats as well as opportunities as humanitarianism is 'redefined and placed centre stage'.

For critics like Macrae and de Torrente, the pursuit of policy coherence has led to results that are questionable on grounds both of ethics and efficacy. Others take a more sanguine view. Michael Ignatieff[17] writes 'Humanitarian action is not unmasked if it is shown to be the instrument of political power. Motives are not discredited just because they are shown to be mixed'. The worry, perhaps, is rather that a true convergence of agendas is rare; and that too often, political agendas dictate forms of action that are simply at odds with humanitarian principles.

Aggressive Humanitarianism and the Responsibility to Protect

Traditionally, and as articulated in the Geneva Conventions, humanitarianism embodies a doctrine of restraint in the use of force. It defines certain categories of people and things as 'protected' and then requires of belligerents that they exercise restraint in the waging of war. The guiding principles here are distinction between military and civilian targets, and precaution/proportionality in the use of force. Recent year have seen the evolution of what might be called aggressive humanitarianism—that is, calls for the use of force on humanitarian grounds— that sits uneasily with the traditional notion of restraint. The use of the term 'humanitarian war' to describe the Kosovo campaign, for example, caused deep unease to many humanitarian agencies, not just to the ICRC. The evolution of this strand of thought can be traced both at the political level (e.g. in the UN Security Council) and in the rhetoric of some humanitarian agencies. While calls for the use of force may be more or less prescriptive as to the type of military action required, they all share the same basic rationale. The call to 'protect' has largely gone from being a plea for restraint in the use of force to a call for force to be deployed by third parties. While this has a certain logic to it—effective protection will sometimes depend on the use of force—it is a potentially dangerous logic, given the broad (and not necessarily humanitarian) interpretation given to 'protection', the inevitable political selectivity surrounding intervention, and the highly variable effectiveness of such interventions in the past. Depending on one's point of view, this trend can be seen either as a political maturing of the humanitarian agenda or a worrying loss of humanitarian perspective.

The recent revival of 'just war' doctrine since the end of the Cold War, and particularly at the time of the Kosovo invasion, has seen it refashioned in something like a humanitarian mould. The so-called 'Clinton Doctrine' is echoed in the pre-millennial (and pre-9/11) rhetoric of UK Prime Minister Tony Blair[18] who in relation to Kosovo articulated criteria for intervention that included, but did not privilege, the pursuit of national interest in the form of state security ('This is a just war, based not on any territorial ambitions but on values'). The 2001 report of the Canadian-sponsored International Commission on Intervention and State Sovereignty (The Responsibility to Protect) adopts just war principles still more explicitly, and is the most comprehensive formulation of the emerging doctrine of humanitarian intervention.[19] The extent to which these new formulations are consistent with a traditional humanitarian perspective is debatable. Certainly the criteria by which wars are judged 'just' extend well beyond humanitarian criteria.[20] Most important, perhaps, is the question of whether calling for the use of force can be justified on humanitarian grounds, given the traditional focus (of IHL) on restraint in the use of force. The latter remains central, and the use of force to 'protect' carries with it the potential for causing harm which in some cases can be devastating: see for example the Iraq civilian mortality survey conducted by Les Roberts and his colleagues.[21]

The attitude of INGOs on these questions has been ambivalent. Mindful of their collective failure in Bosnia to put civilian protection at the heart of the humanitarian agenda, and of the charge that they acted as 'fig-leaves' for political inaction there and in the Great Lakes, many have in recent years become more inclined to accept or to call for the use of force on humanitarian grounds. But many of these same agencies have in practice subsequently complained at the blurring of military/civil assistance roles on the ground,[22] though they have been less forceful critics of the failure to protect by mandated forces such as the United Nations Organization Mission in Democratic Republic of the Congo. They have sometimes accepted (indeed depended upon) military protection for their own operations, yet find their operating space apparently closing down in part, they argue, because of association with those same forces and their political masters. Even those like the ICRC who accept no such protection are increasingly restricted in contexts like Afghanistan, and find themselves the deliberate target of insurgents for whom they represent the enemy regime—and a soft target for attack.

Conclusion

This chapter has sketched some of the divergence in INGO approaches revealed by shifts in the international political sphere. Is one position more truly humanitarian than the other? Not necessarily. While agencies squabble over which is the path of righteousness, others welcome the diversity of approaches.[23] The acid test is actual outcomes; and humanitarian outcomes depend largely on political actions. That being so, the question of how the humanitarian ethic informs public policy becomes at least as important as the way in which it informs agency policies, and arguably much more so. The danger for the INGOs is that proximity to political agendas necessarily involves forms of compromise that may undermine the very rationale of humanitarian action, leaving civilian populations exposed while potentially putting their own staff at risk. There is enough evidence of this tendency from contexts like Angola, Democratic Republic of the Congo, Iraq and Afghanistan to take the charge extremely seriously. It has a bearing on the role of the UN—in which the humanitarian and other agendas are uniquely combined—and the attitude of INGOs to UN-led co-ordination models. While those issues lie beyond the scope of this paper, they are the subject of increasingly animated discussion among practitioners. For the people affected by these decisions, the issues involved are not theoretical but absolutely real.

PART 4

HUMANITARIANISM AND RELIGION

It is said that when the Roman Empire was ravaged by the plague in the third century, Christians remained amongst the dying—an extreme gesture of solidarity drawing its strength from religious texts such as the Gospel according to Saint John, which proclaimed that 'God is love', the love that is translated as 'caritas' or charity. Often a benchmark for a good conscience, charity forms the basis of modern humanitarianism, whatever the 'French doctors', nourished at the breast of anticlericalism, would like to believe. What are the links between religions and humanitarianism today? Are ancient texts still at the root of denominational NGOs and do Islamist NGOs act as cover for terrorist networks? Christophe Courtin and Adeel Jafferi set out to answer these questions, in an effort to reconcile the spiritual and the temporal.

9

CHRISTIAN NGOS ON THE INTERNATIONAL SCENE

WHAT ARE THEIR MOTIVES?

Christophe Courtin

In the wake of the Second Vatican Council in 1967, the Chair of Caritas Internationalis wrote as an epigraph to the French translation of the encyclical letter Populorum Progressio 'Today, the social question is a global question'. Was Pope Paul VI one of the first anti-globalisation campaigners? He even stated, 'We earnestly urge all men to pool their ideas and their activities for man's complete development and the development of all mankind'.[1] It could not be much clearer. Today many Catholic NGOs define their mission statements in line with this spiritual tradition. This message is particularly pertinent today, when civil society worldwide is questioning the meaning of the new geopolitical nature of human existence, commonly termed 'globalisation'. The choice to work for the poorest was strongly reaffirmed by Pope John Paul II throughout his pontificate and has always been one of the pillars of action by Catholics at international level. Of course, denominational associations, including Catholic ones, which claim faith as the basis of their action, do not all follow this path. Some still see religious proselytising as the motive for their action. However, it is clear that the historical and intellectual trajectory that led to this founding commitment, built on an optimistic view of humanity, is

101

MANY REASONS TO INTERVENE

common to all NGOs that intervene on the international stage on the basis of defending the dignity of man, whether they are denominational or not. Starting from this premise and excluding religious organisations whose purpose is to convert, do denominational NGOs have a motive that is specific to them for acting internationally? Even if they do, this specific motive is not a clear criterion for making a distinction between organisations. It is an indicator, even an index, of the individual motivations of adherents within these organisations. The suspicion of rampant proselytising held by some organisations that claim to be secular is less and less replicated in the wider family of international humanitarian organisations.

The Anthropological Question

Still on the subject of the Catholic Church, one can point out that, as early as the sixteenth century, the Dominican Las Casas was defending the rights of Indians on the one hand, while on the other the Pope was giving his blessing to the deportation of Africans to the West Indies— early signs of globalisation. In the nineteenth century, Catholic missionaries arrived in the cargo holds of colonial armies. During the dark years in Latin America, priests and even bishops were among the ranks of social militants fighting for human rights, whilst military chaplains were on board the Argentinean planes from which political prisoners were thrown into the sea, their hands tied behind their backs. The debate is familiar: how can you reconcile your Christian values to intervene in development or humanitarian action when, in the name of these same values, your Church has covered up, and may have participated in, numerous human rights abuses perpetrated by those in power? This controversial issue is regularly raised in a caricature fashion by those who do not understand that personal and militant commitment in development and humanitarian action is more often based on the question of meaning, of acting for others, than on the institutional identity of the organisation that represents that commitment. One could object that there is no need to have faith or to belong to a religious group to question the meaning of life. True enough; but when the question about the meaning of life is asked, the metaphysical question is never far away.

Before addressing this metaphysical question: what exists beyond nature, beyond real and observable facts (private questions which are not the subject of this paper), humanitarian organisations first ask anthropological questions: should we act towards and for others; what is man's purpose; what is the function of mankind? All members of international humanitarian organisations, religious or not, ask themselves these kinds of questions. Answers given by organisations to their teams are more or less comprehensive and clear, depending on whether they are based on a body of doctrine or are ideas constructed by the institution and its history. Obviously, in the case of Christian organisations, the answers to both the anthropological and metaphysical questions are well explored and documented. However, when all is said and done, it is a view of man and mankind, a moral philosophy and ethical code, which has structured the history of international action by humanitarian organisations, that still enables us to understand the foundation of their policies.

Let us first exclude denominational organisations that base their action on religious practice or a literal interpretation of religious texts. Although they are present and visible on the humanitarian scene, their influence is limited to their beneficiaries, who are recruited almost systematically in proportion to the resources these organisations have at their disposal to provide aid. These resources are sometimes plentiful and are often mobilised through large charity campaigns led by churches or religious organisations. In the case of Islam, charity is one of the pillars of the faith. However, these organisations do not aim to act directly in the political sphere, content to simply help their flock or their future partners in faith. One can legitimately question the fundamental motives of these actions, but one should not underestimate their impact. In some cases, they relieve real suffering, but they also have a real influence on the local socio-economic context and therefore on policy. However, these organisations are not within the scope of this paper, which reviews denominational organisations that base their motivation for international action on their ethics, rather than on a moral code drawn from a religious perception of man.

Humanitarianism and Religion: An Ancient and Fundamental Relationship?

In more concrete terms, it is easy to identify the perception of mankind held by Henri Dunant, the founder of the Red Cross, and that of the 'French doctors' and emergency relief actors in general. It is built around an optimistic view of human beings, their dignity and liberty and individual freedom, their physical and moral integrity, regardless of nationality, race or religion. This view of mankind is based on humanism, i.e. on an understanding of anthropological questions, which denominational organisations also ask themselves. In the Western history of ideas, this humanism expressed itself in the form of human rights, the liberalism of the Enlightenment, which aimed to rid itself of the institutional control of both the State and the Catholic Church, and asserted the existence of individual and universal rights. Going back further in time, humanism was itself partly the product of a more ancient Christian humanism which dates back to the Renaissance, before the wars of religion, of which Erasmus is one of the most emblematic figures. Going back even further, the founding texts of Christianity contain calls for tolerance, charity, respect for others, whoever they are, forming a basis of religious humanism. The Gospels contain numerous references to a view of mankind that participates in denominational organisations, as well as secular international humanitarian organisations.

Following the course of the history of ideas in the other direction, one can see that Catholic organisations inspired by Populorum Progressio (1967) branched off from the central-liberal movement symptomatic of the mid-nineteenth century European revolutions, when Catholic thinkers and religious congregations were reflecting on a new Catholic and social humanism. Pre-Marxist socialism originated from this branch, which was soon to link up with ideas of 'Republic' and 'democracy', leading to Catholic action movements engaged in development with the creation of the CCFD at the time of the Second Vatican Council, opening up of the church to modernisation. In the second half of the twentieth century, the fusion of Marxist sociology with Catholic spirituality gave rise, mainly in Latin America, to liberation theology, which today is undergoing new developments. The liberal movement also had its own history, particularly English, and trod the line between continental idealism and Anglo-Saxon pragmatism. Financial marketing and calls for donations using compassionate advertising, techniques implemented by emergency relief organisations, also have their roots in this history of ideas. In France, the term *humanitaire* itself was historically constructed in the nineteenth century, when its status changed from an adjective to a noun. Today, it has lost a little of its substance because, to the wider public, it covers both the actions of emergency relief organisations and those of development organisations. In French, the term *organisation de solidarité internationale* ('international solidarity organisation') is now preferred to the term 'humanitarian organisation'.

This long and necessary—yet incomplete—detour through the history and sources of the founding values of modern thinking simply aims to demonstrate that it is not possible to answer the question of humanitarianism and religion without taking account of these complex historical constructions. Political or religious currents of ideas and thoughts, non-religious or religious ideologies and the contributions of social sciences, form a tangled web that is almost impossible to deconstruct.

During meetings convened in response to international developments that have repercussions on human rights—as in Colombia, Palestine and Sri Lanka, for example—an external observer would be unable to distinguish the words of an activist from Secours Catholique or the CCFD from those of one from Agir Ici or Secours Populaire. Should one conclude that denomination is no longer a useful criterion for analysing international humanitarian organisations? Viewed in terms of the perception of mankind upheld by organisations operating in secularised European societies, that is arguably the case. This view is now commonly shared at a time when religion is kept away from politics. However, the religious criterion still has a particular relevance in the context of debates surrounding the mode of intervention.

How to Intervene?

The choice of acting for the poorest, which is constantly reaffirmed by the Catholic Church, enables it to put all its weight into denouncing the scandalous inequalities that exist around the world, yet it does not propose a mode of intervention in the social or political field. The encyclical letter Populorum Progressio provides this for Catholic NGOs. They still put into practice this fundamental principle which comes from the philosophy of the Dominican priest Joseph Lebret, who inspired the encyclical letter, and according to which, the development of mankind and that of peoples are integrally linked. It is therefore impossible to act on organisations without acting on the individual, and vice versa. Development aid cannot be understood without education about development. The 'here' and the 'there' interact and understand each other, pressure must be put on the structures, both social and intellectual, to fight poverty and under-development. For their part, emergency relief organisations which arose out of conflicts resulting from the international crises of the 1970s, and in response to the lack of humanitarian aid in states faced with natural disasters, have developed modes of action based on political neutrality, logistical efficiency and the practical and immediate response to suffering. Today, the divide between emergency relief organisations that intervene in situations of armed conflict and natural disasters on the one hand, and development organisations on the other, is not as clear-cut. All international humanitarian organisations know that it is impossible to have an influence on consequences without at some point addressing causes. Depending on their resources, their competencies or their history, they will instead intervene to change the consequences or the causes of violations of human dignity. It is in these modes of intervention that some of the motives of Christian organisations can be identified.

Since Porto Alegre in January 2001, the dynamic has been inspired by the process of the World Social Forum. Initiated by a small nucleus of Brazilian associations it brought together trade unionists, human rights activists and social actors, some of them practising Catholics. During the dark years in Latin America, the Catholic Church was one of the rare places of protection for progressive activists, and this melting pot gave rise to an in-depth reflection on the links between social struggles and Christian spirituality. This movement, which cannot be reduced to liberation theology, shaped the groups of activists that can be found today in the ranks of anti-globalisation campaigners who propose a radical critique of neo-liberalism and its consequences for the rise in inequalities in the world. Many international Catholic humanitarian organisations were present at the last World Social Forum.

In the spectrum of civil society organisations operating at global level, their political analyses identify them more with traditional trade unions and activist left-wing associations than with organisations that fight against poverty within the framework of major institutional donor programmes, or that intervene in humanitarian disasters through exclusively public funding. NGOs such as Secours Catholique, the evangelical Protestant missionary society DÉFAP or ASMAE (the Sister Emmanuelle Association) believe that the fight against poverty cannot be limited to enhancing the solvency of the least poor of the poor, to give them access to the market, leaving those excluded from the path of economic development to the care and compassion of humanitarian charities. Enlarging Malthus' banquet table is not sufficient; each guest must move a little to leave room for their neighbour. These NGOs believe that the fight against poverty also involves a fight against the inequalities aggravated by contemporary economic liberalism. This fight must be carried out in accordance with democratic rules. At Porto Alegre, apart from the large British reformist organisations, traditional humanitarian organisations descended from the 'French doctors' were barely represented. This political approach to intervention on the causes of under-development is characteristic of Christian organisations, which see their ideas through to the end, in defence of human dignity.

Catholic Organisations and AIDS

Health is the main intervention area of international humanitarian organisations. It mobilises the largest proportion of resources and it is also the most visible. It would therefore be lacking in courage in a paper that attempts to analyse the motivation for the international action of Catholic humanitarian organisations on the basis of their view of mankind to avoid the controversy surrounding AIDS that was revived by Pope Benedict XVI during his visit to Cameroon in March 2009.

Here again, the debate is familiar. On this subject, the views of the most determined critics of the Catholic Church are clear: the Catholic moral stance against the use of condoms, which are the best protection against the spread of the disease, is irresponsible in the extreme. For those who, like this author, have lived in Africa, worked in health centres and lost several friends to the disease, the accusation is a tough one. When he declared, during the flight taking him to Africa for his first visit as Pope in March 2009, that the use of condoms aggravated the problem, the Pope shocked many European Catholics and particularly those in the frontline of health programmes working to fight against AIDS. Paradoxically this debate is much milder, if not to say non-existent amongst African Catholics.

During his pontificate, John Paul II, a philosopher and specialist in Christian phenomenology, was aware of the disruption caused by the issues of sexual morals, the development of our scientific knowledge of life and technological advances in genetic manipulation on our perception of the phenomenon of life. These theological arguments were constructed for him by Pope Benedict XVI, then Cardinal Ratzinger. In Christian churches and in Catholicism, ideological approaches to these issues are not set in stone; they are still changing, in spite of the Pope's recent comments. The ethics of the Catholic hierarchy have a very strong philosophical basis, a vision of life against which no violation can be justified by human action. This overwhelming line of defence explains the position of Catholic thinkers on abortion, human cloning, contraception, the death penalty and the 'patentability' of the living. On these last two points, studies show that Catholic humanitarian organisations are in tune with the hierarchy. The radical stance adopted by the Catholic Church on contraception should be understood in this context, rather than as a new manifestation of the fundamental conservatism of the Catholic establishment. Like all ethical systems, however, this one is contingent on reality and social power relations: it is always under construction. The dividing line between the end of the answer to the question concerning the nature of life and the beginning of the answer to the anthropological question of dealing with the dignity of human beings and their suffering in the face of death, is not final. Networks of Catholic intellectuals, clerical and secular, are actively studying, outside all debate, this serious issue which is at the frontier of theology, ethics and human reality. We can't say that the wind is blowing in their favour at the moment.

All the while, AIDS continues to wreak havoc. Threatened populations will not wait for theologians or philosophers to elaborate the Church's doctrine and produce answers that are adapted to their situation. In everyday practice, many religious NGOs that find themselves on the front line of this drama and advocate chastity, fidelity and responsible sexual behaviour to fight against this curse, also daily adopt a very pragmatic pastoral approach to condoms to deal with the situation. This could be considered sheer hypocrisy were it not for the large number of denominational international humanitarian organisations fighting for the recognition of the rights of HIV-positive patients and their free access to antiretroviral therapies. In spite of everything, Pope Benedict has increased the pressure on African Catholic organisations working in the field of health. Awareness raising meetings about the use of condoms that these organisations have available to run in parishes are now more difficult to arrange, they depend on the independence and courage of some priests. The Pope's position is a harsh blow. When one knows that the main cause of death of priests in

Africa is AIDS, it could be said that, one day, the reality of life will catch up with this archaic, doctrinaire position on the condom. Finally, the actions of the teams of denominational humanitarian NGOs are not different in essence from those of their secular colleagues. For many militant believers, practising their faith cannot be separated from the defence of human rights, from which they draw their motivation.

10

IS THERE AN ISLAMIC HUMANITARIANISM?

Adeel Jafferi

In the aftermath of the terrorist attack on the World Trade Center, the war in Afghanistan and then the war in Iraq, humanitarian actors have faced unprecedented hostility and peril. However, of all humanitarian NGOs affected by the recent political events subsequent to 9/11, none have been more influenced than Islamic charities. With attention focused on the Islamic world, some have argued that it is incumbent upon Muslims to set the record straight.

Islam is accused of being a religion that is based on conquest and violence; that it is incumbent upon Muslims to gain greater adherents to their faith, even if this means using the sword as a weapon of conversion. This accusation, despite its inherent fallacy, has blighted Muslims, as much in the course of their everyday lives, as in the humanitarian field. The accusations of using humanitarianism to proselytise misses the point of the valuable work carried out by Muslims in this field. The fact that there are many Islamic NGOs who do proselytise in the same way as many non-Muslim NGOs do, does not allow for recognition of those who consider missionary work as much an anathema as do many non-Muslim faith based or secular aid organisations.

The proud tradition of humanitarianism amongst Muslims is only now receiving widespread recognition. It has taken a great deal of effort on the part of Islamic NGOs to attain a degree of respect and this effort continues where in certain quarters there is still some suspicion and scepticism about the quality and, indeed the motives, of Muslims in the humanitarian field. NGOs throughout the Muslim world, such as Islamic Relief have worked ceaselessly in the humanitarian field and have made great strides to challenge the underlying doubts as well as the traditional monopoly enjoyed by Western faith-based and, more recently, secular NGOs. Although Islamic NGOs have really only tentatively been acknowledged in the same breath as organisations such as Oxfam, the fact is that humanitarianism has played a large part since the early days of Islamic theological and imperial expansion.

Charity in Islam

The very pillars of Islam make it incumbent on every Muslim to help others. This principle is so strong that it is mentioned time again in the Qur'an, the Muslim holy book. Indeed, God says in the Qur'an: 'I only accept prayer from he who has mercy upon the poor, the wayfarer, the widow and the injured'.

Muslims strive to gain the blessings and goodwill of God and are required to use the earth's resources responsibly. This stewardship plays a key part in the life of a Muslim. It is their mission as humans to show respect and appreciation for others by working for a better future.

It is important to remind ourselves that over half the funds received by Muslim organisations come from *Zakat* contributions. *Zakat* is a levy on the property of the wealthy for distribution to society's poor. The Arabic word '*Zakat*' has connotations of purity, increase, and blessing and paying it purifies, increases, blesses, and blesses the remainder of one's wealth. *Zakat* is 2.5 per cent of all zakatable wealth one possesses in a lunar year. If the wealth amounts to less than a threshold figure—the '*nisab*'—then no *Zakat* is payable. This threshold limit is 87.48g of gold, or its equivalent in cash. *Zakat* donors usually leave it for Islamic NGOs where the money is spent to allow the scope of charity to be maximised. Charitable deeds are considered a particularly blessed act: 'Allah and His angels, the people of heaven and earth, even the ant on his anthill and the fish in the sea, pray for those who teach goodness to humanity' (Hadith).

Islam teaches the importance of helping others. This becomes clearer during Ramadan when Muslims throughout the world fast. In doing so they strive to empathise with the starving and the destitute. Beyond Ramadan, the principles of *Sadaqah* and *Zakat* provide two of the most important Islamic precepts. They involve giving a portion of one's own savings to those in need, in order to create a more just and equitable world. Much has been written about these particular Islamic tenets, but a third element, *Waqf*, also needs to be discussed to understand the process of charity which Islam advocates in perpetuity.

Waqf is a type of continuous charity, which can be a gift of money or property, can be used to bring a charitable return, but cannot be sold. The Prophet Mohammed regarded *Waqf* as the best form of charity and created *Waqf* himself as well as encouraging his companions and followers to do the same. Since the time of the Prophet, *Waqf* generally took the form of donated property or an institution that helped others. For example, houses were converted to inns for travellers and waterways were built to direct water towards villages. During the time of the Ottoman Empire the income generated from over 20,000 *Waqf* was equal to a third of the state's wealth.

Threats to Islamic Charities

In the past four decades there has been a dramatic increase in the number of Islamic NGOs in the East and West which have embarked upon vital and high profile humanitarian relief work.

Islamic NGOs in the West are a relatively new phenomenon and for that reason are still finding their way through the minefield of political dialectic which so often affects humanitarian work. This has, unfortunately, meant that they are also easier to manipulate and forced to take decisions based not always on sound humanitarian bases but for political ones which affect their very survival. The level of government involvement in humanitarian work is counter to the concept of non-governmental organisations. For the sake of institutional funding, however, NGOs have had to get into bed with those who, some argue, they should keep at a greater distance. In the case of Islamic NGOs this has been added to by the greater need for legitimacy and credibility, essential for their very survival.

Since 9/11, however, many Islamic governments have been forced to close their doors after veiled comments by Western governments that they are being used to fund terrorist networks. As a knee-jerk reaction, charities carrying out vital humanitarian work have had their work unnecessarily and disastrously curtailed.

One of the main developments since the events of 11 September 2001 has been the clamping down of Islamic charities, particularly in Muslim countries. As a result of 'gentle persuasion' by some Western governments and the accusations that some NGOs have been financially supporting terrorist networks, many governments in the Muslim world have imposed blanket bans on Islamic NGOs. This has had disastrous consequences for humanitarian work and, conversely, has the potential to have the opposite of the desired effect. In Islam, as mentioned earlier, charitable donations are obligatory on all Muslims. Whereas in the past, people have donated their *Zakat* through bona fide NGOs, with the restrictions on these organisations, individuals are forced to pay *Zakat* away from the scrutiny of the regulatory bodies that, in one form or another, exist to ensure transparency and accountability.

The result of this is that the laundering of money—the threat of which resulted in the closing of these charities—is far easier to achieve, as well as the diverting of money for nefarious reasons. The dangerous corollary of this has been that only non-Muslim charities have been able to operate effectively in countries such as Iraq, where suspicions of Western institutions are at dangerously high levels. NGOs are often seen as alternative arms of the Western military or intelligence agencies.

In a meeting of 160 NGO's at the annual Interaction Forum in Washington on the 17 May 2004, issues of security were discussed and it was agreed by attendees that perceptions amongst the Muslim community were a critical issue. With some beneficiaries unable to distinguish between 'humanitarian aid' being delivered by military personnel with weapons, contractors with weapons and NGOs with armed protection the line blurs between military personnel and civilian aid workers.

This has had catastrophic consequences. The bombings of the UN and Red Cross Headquarters in Baghdad have dealt severe blows to humanitarian relief efforts with many aid agencies leaving either only a token presence in some countries or leaving altogether.

This suspicion should assist Islamic NGOs in that they should be considered legitimate humanitarian organisations, untainted by Western government infiltration. This has not necessarily been the case, however. The very fact that Islamic NGOs are allowed to operate has been seen by some as proof that they are part of the establishment that is perceived to be persecuting them. Their transparency, rather than being a positive factor, has led to suspicions amongst some Muslims that they are working for that same establishment. This could have major security implications for staff and beneficiaries. If Muslims are under suspicion, one can only imagine how great the difficulties must be for non-Muslim aid workers.

Another consequence has been that as there are so few Western Muslim NGOs implementing humanitarian projects, the pressure on those that remain is overwhelming. Both logistically and financially it is becoming increasingly difficult to cope with the needs of beneficiaries. Their needs are in danger of not being met. This will inevitably lead to greater discontent in the Muslim community and the world at large. This will remain the case even if the few Islamic NGOs are currently working in the humanitarian field are offered financial support from the international community. The current situation is such that aid agencies who have been forced to close down their operations in countries such as Afghanistan, Palestine Iraq, Pakistan and many others, have left in their wake millions of people with no hope of support from any other than non-legitimate organisations. These people are the losers and are potential recruits to the growing army of discontented Muslims who are cynically targeted by those with nefarious and deadly agendas. Adding to the growing numbers of those who feel abandoned are the countless thousands of local NGO employees whose incomes were often the only source of revenue for whole communities. The consequent disruption to local economies is devastating. The lack of employment opportunities and regular incomes has often been cited as a potential factor in the recruiting of civilians for terrorist purposes.

The ultimate losers in these attempts at controlling transfers of money will be the beneficiaries, the donors and governments—in the East and the West—who will face a backlash from their citizens. It also makes the work of Western NGOs much harder because they will be met with suspicion and hostility as well as the jealousy of those Islamic NGOs who have been marginalised in their favour.

In a post-9/11 world, humanitarians find it more difficult to operate as they are often targeted because of misconceived perceptions that they are carrying out clandestine policies of Western governments. With the devastating effects of the bombings of UN and Red Cross Headquarters in Baghdad as well as attacks on NGOs in other countries, the work of humanitarians has never been more difficult. Add to this the alarming spate of kidnappings of aid workers in Iraq and Afghanistan, and the situation has never been more critical. The ultimate losers as a result of this are, ironically, the very people who terrorists claim that they wish to help. NGOs have been forced to abandon the very people who stand to gain the most from humanitarian intervention.

After the earthquake in Bam, in Iran at the end of 2003, Islamic Relief was heavily involved in the relief efforts and facilitated the work of a large number of other NGOs who faced difficulties in a usually insular society. The dire need for humanitarian intervention necessitated a breaking down of barriers on the side of humanitarians and the Iranian authorities. The beauty of working in Iran was that it was the first time for many, from Iran and from the West, to actually meet and begin to understand each other, thereby beginning the process of contact which, one will hope, will eventually lead to reconciliation and bridge-building.

The positive effect that humanitarian actors can have on the perceptions, at least amongst the affected populations, is incalculable. It was gratifying, in the wake of such a major catastrophe to see Americans and Iranians, who since the Islamic Revolution of 1979 have had negative perceptions of one another, coming together and learning about each other's cultures, beliefs and aspirations. This positive consequence of such a major disaster cannot be overstated. The NGO community acted as a bridge between two seemingly diametrically opposed cultures and was able to achieve diplomatic strides which even ambassadors and recognised diplomats have often found impossible.

The Capacity of Muslim NGOs and Co-ordination with Non-Muslim

Islamic Relief works in non-Muslim areas and has never distinguished between the delivery of aid on the basis of a potential beneficiary's faith. The Prophet once said to his companions that 'He is not one of us who goes to bed on a full stomach while his neighbour is hungry'. He did not say whether the neighbour was Muslim or non-Muslim and this is a strong pervading principle throughout the work of NGOs like Islamic Relief. Islamic Relief has worked amongst Hindu and Buddhist populations in India and Sri Lanka as well as amongst Christians in many other parts of the world. However, many Islamic NGOs work under the premise that many, if not most of the humanitarian crises of our day, be they natural or man-made—are happening in the Muslim world. By definition, therefore, they feel that they are best suited to be at the vanguard of the humanitarian response. Part of the reason for this is the assumption that non-Muslim NGOs have a covert agenda to influence Muslim cultures either in the political or religious spheres. In the current crisis in Sudan, for example, Darfurians stated to me that they are no longer able to distinguish between Muslims and Arabs. By extension, they say, if the *Janjaweed*—the so-called Arab militias which have targeted them for violence—are Muslims then they do not wish to be considered Muslims. This has had a great deal of resonance amongst the Islamic aid community. Organisations like the Saudi Red Crescent Society are currently setting up medical relief operations throughout the region. Whilst their intention is to help in the alleviation of the suffering of innocent people caught up in a conflict not of their making, it would be true to say that they are also attempting to redress the negative impression which has been created in the minds of the people of Darfur. This is an impression, Muslims feel, which has been reinforced by the media and by political rhetoric in the West.

The Western NGO community, Western governments, international development agencies and United Nations organisations have not helped. In many countries, particularly in my experience where central government is weak, there is a certain degree of 'them and us' in respect of Islamic NGOs. In Sudan, for example, there is an element of Islamic organisations being marginalised when it comes to co-ordination of relief efforts and when it comes to institutional funding for projects in the field.

On the other hand, there are those Islamic NGOs who are unwilling to recognise their own limitations and often will respond to emergencies because of a well-intentioned, but ultimately misguided, attempt to be seen to be doing something. In their eyes it enhances their credibility in the eyes of their donors and the wider Muslim community. However, this lack of a serious understanding of how the wider aid community works proves a danger not only to themselves, but also to the affected communities they seek to assist.

In terms of official credibility and legitimacy very few Islamic humanitarian NGOs have received positive endorsements from governments and from the general non-Islamic NGO community. In maintaining their traditional links and the support and respect of their core donor group, Islamic NGOs have had to make certain sacrifices. The main one has, of course, been recognition from their non-Muslim counterparts. The situation where there has been the most contention has been in the realm of advocacy. Islamic Relief is only now, after twenty years of existence, tentatively dipping its toe into an area which non-Muslim NGOs have been involved in for many years with a large measure of success. In building strong relations with Western governments and with their non-Islamic counterparts, Islamic Relief has been able to harness their strength and make bold statements of a political nature. This has led to recent ventures in the area of peace-building which have gained a certain degree of success and are expected to lead to greater approaches in this very difficult area.

Christian Aid, Cafod and Caritas are just some of the many faiths inspired agencies with whom Islamic Relief has worked in close and successful collaboration over its twenty year existence. This co-operation is the cornerstone of Islamic Relief and provides yet another example of how people of all cultures, throughout the world can do so much good when they unite in the cause of humanity. Faith, unity and co-operation are the driving factors behind successes in this field. The ultimate goal is to help others. The need for tolerance and respect for those of a different or no faith is made more relevant when we consider that disunity in the field will only prevent desperately needed work being carried out effectively and with success.

To achieve so much in so few years has not always been easy. Many Muslims in the UK have at times felt isolated and voices in favour of Islamic values and the positive Muslim contribution to British Society have been few. However, despite such grave events as the Gulf Wars and the terrible atrocity on 11 September 2001, the Muslim community—both humanitarian and civilian—far from being compelled to isolate themselves have actually grown in strength and popularity. This is a great tribute, both to the British people of whom Muslims are a proud part, but also of the understanding and tolerance of human beings in general.

Conclusion

In the last decades, the Muslim community in the UK has grown significantly. Muslims have increasingly entered mainstream society, in politics, business, diplomacy, media and of course in the humanitarian field. Countrywide, Mosques and Islamic Schools have opened their doors to new generations of British Muslims—reinforcing the message of tolerance and moderation advocated by Islam. Equally gratifyingly, British Muslims have also retained links with their countries of origin, enhancing all our lives with the best of these rich and diverse Muslim cultures. This has contributed on both sides to new levels of understanding between the Muslim and non-Muslim world.

Islamic NGOs are uniquely positioned to bridge the gap between the East and the West which exist in today's society. At Islamic Relief, for example, as a humanitarian aid agency founded and run on Muslim principles we have, over the years, received overwhelming support from Muslim communities throughout the world. They are familiar with our work and our ethos; they recognise our credentials as humanitarians and Muslims. As a British charity, we have been able to show the principles of charity to a community which has, particularly recently, seen only the worst of Muslims.

Islamic charities can offer a realistic, truthful and unthreatening view of Islam. Our role is as humanitarians, but we also have a duty to bring people together. The true meaning of charity in Islam is helping others regardless of race, creed or colour. We have provided aid to millions, but in our small way, we have also, I believe, been able to change some of negative stereotypes about Muslims prevalent amongst many in society.

Today, many people of the world see Islam as a threat to their way of life. The truth is, however, that they are being influenced by the actions and the rhetoric—religious and political—of a small minority of Muslims. It is, therefore, incumbent upon Muslims, through action, not just rhetoric, to reinforce to the world that their aspirations and skill in helping the needy are as great as anybody else in the humanitarian field.

EPILOGUE

David Rieff

While it is of course self-evident that humanitarian action long predates Biafra, and that there had long been deep support, if narrow among church-goers for the caritative work of missionaries, it was in Biafra in 1968 that humanitarian action first started to capture the popular imagination of masses of people in Western Europe and North America. The editors of this book refer to this in their introduction, and refer to humanitarianism's 'twenty glorious years' from the Nigerian Civil War to the end of the Cold War. They are right, at least in the sense that during this period independent relief groups succeeded establishing themselves as important actors on the international scene, even, if, as subsequent experience would prove, the reality was that they were neither as important nor as independent as they briefly came to imagine themselves to be. And that rise came bearing at least one national stereotype in its talons—the image of the 'French Doctors' that was so sedulously promoted by Bernard Kouchner both in Biafra before the creation of MSF and during his comparatively brief though incredibly histrionic and hectic leadership of that organisation.

National stereotypes in any domain are hard to resist, but they are harder still either to really get right or to derive anything of value from. At best, we should probably say about such cultural typecasting what Nietzsche said about history—that while we may need it, 'But not the way the spoiled loafer in the garden of knowledge needs it'. There are real historical distinctions to be drawn between the origins of humanitarian action in Britain and in France. As anyone can see simply by

121

spending some time on the websites of, say, MSF France and Oxfam UK, there are indeed real differences in cultural styles as well, and they are expertly delineated by Rony Brauman in his preface, that can be said to at least partly transcend particular institutional and ideological dependencies, the obligations, and the commitments that they bring to their work of any particular NGO, whether British or French.

As most of the contributors to this book emphasise, these distinctions should not be exaggerated. Style and substance may not be wholly discrete categories but nor are they exactly the same thing either. And when people speak, as they routinely do, which makes this volume with its sober reserve on the question all the more valuable, of the gulf between French and British approaches, often what they in fact are really saying is the gap between MSF France and not only their British, American, German, and Scandinavian counterparts, but their French ones as well. That attitude of being partly outside the humanitarian system is one that MSF France cultivated from the start, though in those early days the group's *compromesso storico* with the International Committee of the Red Cross would probably not have been expected.

In the field, it is routine to hear other NGOs complain about MSF France's 'go it alone' attitude, insisting that it is both arrogant and counter-productive. To anyone who knows Britain at all, it will be immediately apparent that recapitulated here is bog standard British Francophobia (there is British Francophilia as well, of course, but one finds few people with the attitudes of a Julian Barnes at Save the Children or Oxfam in the UK). One can speculate that because, apart from MSF, the origins of most of the major relief NGOs of equal size are to be found either in Britain or in Holland, Germany, Scandinavia, and the US, where, whatever else divides NGOs from these countries, close co-operation with government and the United Nations system and a profound commitment to the idea that NGOs should be involved in both relief and development (and, more recently, with human rights), that this rather British attitude has become the default position of NGOs and UN agencies when they come into conflict with MSF—as at one point or another, they generally do.

This selfish, bloody-minded, boastful, non-team playing Frenchman versus conformist, servile, do-gooding British human rights activist or government servant disguised as a relief worker dichotomy is the stuff of countless conversations both in the field and in NGO head offices from Aceh to Darfur. But while, in 'long shot', it looks compelling, 'close up', its importance seems greatly diminished. This is not to say that it is unimportant, for the good and sufficient reason that culture, particularly when expressed as cultural hostility, is never without practical implications. But it is not dispositive. It is also, as several contributors to this book show in detail, as much if not more functional as it is cultural. For example, in his contribution, Hugo Slim's essay and boils down less to culture than to the British tendency to view humanitarian aid agencies as of necessity being institutions with multiple mandates. And as Philippe Ryfman shows in his piece, French agencies continue to take a more sceptical view of expanded mandates, even if they too have increasingly assumed them.

In any case, the severe challenges that contemporary humanitarian action faces lie elsewhere, though the separate question of whether or not these challenges constitute a crisis, while a point most contributors to this volume contest is one that in my view should not be dismissed so quickly—above all, the crisis of legitimacy. Indeed, as relief work becomes more and more international, with the older mainline agencies like MSF and Oxfam now having their original French or British identities increasingly superseded by multinational and international ones as well, the old binary Anglo-French opposition seems increasingly anachronistic. The rise of new humanitarian actors, above all the Islamic relief agencies, the subsuming of much relief work in the battle spaces of the so-called war on terror into a 'winning hearts and minds' operation inseparable from the military aims of the NATO countries from which most of the 'legacy' relief groups still hail, and the return of strong states, from Sri Lanka to Ethiopia, intent on controlling both what NGOs do and what they say, and throw the feasibility of the self-mandated human rights project of some British NGOs in particular into doubt, make the differences between British and French humanitarianism seem comparatively trivial.

'The old complaints, the old complaints are best', wrote Samuel Beckett, a man who moved effortlessly between English and French. Where human fate was concerned, presumably he was right. But where humanitarian action is concerned, nothing could be further from the truth. Humanitarianism in the twenty-first century is more likely to have an EU tradition in which elements of what we associate with both the British and the French traditions are fused. We are not going back there, anymore than we are going back to Hastings or Trafalgar. But this does not lessen the need to know how we got to where we are. This volume makes an immense contribution to that understanding. More important still, in explicating the challenge (or the crisis—call it what you will) now faced by what Alex de Waal famously called the Humanitarian International, the authors point the way toward what relief agencies need to debate if they are to fulfill their own operational standards and moral ambitions in the confusions of the new world that is now coming into existence, and more rapidly than many of us ever imagined.

NOTES

2. CRISES OF MATURITY AND TRANSFORMATION
IN FRENCH NGOS

1. David Rieff, *A Bed For the Night: Humanitarianism in crisis*, New York, Simon and Schuster, 2002. For more details upon humanitarian aid history in general, see Philippe Ryfman, *Une histoire de l'humanitaire*, Paris: La Découverte, Repères, 2008. Or see also for NGOs place in humanitarian aid in prospect, Philippe Ryfman 'Non-Governmental organizations an indispensable player of humanitarian aid', International Review of the Red Cross, vol. 89, n° 865, Cambridge (UK) and Geneva, 2007.

2. This is still the case today, with rare exceptions; the government nominates the candidate of its choice as president. However, in general, the nominee usually demonstrates greater independence, such as the current president of French Red Cross (CRF), Jean-François Mattei, formerly a politician who was Minister of Health under President Jacques Chirac and also a well-known and respected doctor, and writer. Moreover, if the president wants to apply for a second term, he needs to make a real election run, especially in the regional and local committees who hold a great power within the organisation.

3. Gérard Chauvy, *La Croix-Rouge dans la guerre, 1935–1947*, Paris: Flammarion, 2000.

4. Now AVSF (i.e. Agronomists and Veterinaries without Borders), after having merged with and other NGO.

5. The letter 'F' added to the acronyms of the NGOs mentioned signifies 'France' so as to specify that it is the French branch which is meant when I speak about trans-national NGOs (TNGO). For more details of what constitutes a TNGO, see Philippe Ryfman, *Les ONG*, Paris: La Découverte, Repères, second edition, 2009, chap. VI

6. Philippe Ryfman, *La question humanitaire*, Paris: Ellipses, 1999

7. J. C. Rufin, 'Pour l'humanitaire. Dépasser le sentiment d'échec', Le Débat, n°105, 1999.

8. CCD, *Argent et organisations de solidarité internationale 2004/2005*, Paris: CCD, 2008, MAE et Coordination SUD, Commission Coopération Développement (CCD) is a joint state/NGO body. 2005 data is the latest available statistical series for the whole community of French NGOs.

9. Ryfman, Op. cit.

10. Serge Cordellier, 'Action humanitaire: démystifier les ONG', *Alternatives Internationales*, n° 2, May 2002. For a fuller development of this subject and the position of other authors, see also Philippe Ryfman, 2009, Op. cit., Ch. IX.

11. Bernard Husson, 'Les ONG: une légitimité en question', in Jean-Pierre Deler (ed.), *ONG et développement. Société, économie, politique*, Paris: Karthala, 1998.

12. Philippe Ryfman, 'Governance and Policies in Non governmental Organizations', in Michel Feher, Gaëlle Krikorian and Yates Mc Kee (eds.), *Non Governmental Politics*, New York: Zone Books, 2007

13. S. Cohen, *La Résistance des Etats*, Paris: Seuil, 2003.

14. CCD, 2008, op. cit.

15. Ibid.

16. Ibid.

17. Data drawn from the 2009 annual reports of the NGOs quoted.

18. Law of 1 August 2003 'relative to patronage of associations and foundations'.

19. See below.

20. Rony Brauman et Sylvie Brunel, 'Les ONG et l'Afrique', Paris: Questions, 2004 internationales, n° 5, La documentation Française.

21. Pascal Dauvin et Johanna Siméant, *Le travail humanitaire. Les acteurs des ONG, du siège au terrain*, Paris: Presses de Sciences Po, 2002.

22. The question was not considered for headquarters staff, notably because of French employment law. The relatively widespread use of volunteers and interns is probably not only the result of the desire to strengthen the anchorage of NGOs in civil society.

23. Law of 23 Feb. 2005. It provides for the conclusion of an 'international solidarity contract'. The combined duration of missions should not exceed six years under this status.

24. Data drawn from the 2007 annual reports of ACF-F, MSF-F and MDM-F. See also, Philippe Ryfman, 2009, Op. cit.

25. See Notes 12 to 14.

26. Viviane Tchernonog, *Le paysage associatif français 2007. Mesures et évolutions*, Paris: Dalloz et Juris Associations, 2007.

27. European Commission Humanitarian Office.

28. Institut Bioforce Développement, *La gouvernance des organisations européennes de solidarité internationale. L'exemple du processus décisionnel d'ouverture et de fermeture de missions*, Lyon: Bioforce, 2003.

29. Especially the logistics, material storage and documentation sectors or even the management of personnel.

30. Even if they do not express this publicly.
31. One of the first initiatives in this direction brought together a group of British and French experts under the leadership of the Centre pour le Dialogue Humanitaire (CDH) of Geneva in 2003, but it could not be followed up.
32. See the debate between Rony Brauman and Hugo Slim in Libération (25 Dec. 2004) under the title 'Les ONG au cœur de la polémique sur l'humanitaire'.

3. ESTABLISHMENT RADICALS: AN HISTORICAL OVERVIEW OF BRITISH NGOS

1. This article deals with the modern forms of charitable action and the reforms of the nineteenth and twentieth centuries. Of course, they existed before this. In the Middle Ages and during the Renaissance, many patrons were responsible for the development of schools, universities, hospitals and foundations, many of which are still with us today.
2. For an overview of the members of the commissions of British NGOs, see www.charitycommission.gov.uk. For more detailed information on the relations between politics and NGOs in the legal context, see publication CC9—Campaigning and political activities.
3. See Ian Bradley, *The Call to Seriousness*, Oxford: Lion Hudson, 2006.
4. Rodney Breen, *Saving Enemy Children: Save the Children's Russian Relief Operation 1921–1923*, in Hugo Slim (ed.), *Children and Childhood in Emergency Policy and Practice, 1919–1924, Disasters*, Oxford: Blackwell.
5. For an excellent outline of the rise of development ideology, see Gilbert Rist, *The History of Development: From Western Origins to Global Faith*, London: Zed Books, 1997.
6. Maggie Black, *A Cause for Our Times: Oxfam—the first fifty years*, Oxford: Oxford University Press, 1992, pp. 156–61.
7. Oxfam, *Words into Action: Basic Rights and the Campaign Against World Poverty*, 1995 and Hugo Slim, *Dissolving the Difference Between Humanitarianism and Development: The Mixing of a Rights-Based Solution*, Development in Practice 10th Anniversary Edition, Oxford: Oxfam, 2000, pp. 491–5.
8. See Tina Wallace et al., *Standardising Development: Influences on UK NGOs' Policies and Practices*, Oxford: Worldview, 1997.
9. ActionAid is the most decentralised NGO, having renounced its British identity and moved its headquarters to South Africa.
10. See Hugo Slim, *By What Authority? The Legitimacy and Accountability of International NGOs*, at www.ichrp.org.
11. See for example the Oxfam UK report Oxfam's Legitimacy and Accountability at www.oxfam.org.uk.

5. EVALUATION FOR CHANGE: HOW CAN WE IMPROVE THE IMPACT OF HUMANITARIAN ACTION?

1. 'Working with complexity and turbulence: Is Sphere the right tool? From technical inconsistencies to recuperation by non-humanitarian actors'; in Charlotte Dufour, François Grünewald, Véronique de Geoffroy, Hugues Maury, Karla Levy (Groupe URD), *Disasters*, Sphere Project, 2002. *Institutionalising Sphere…A great start, next steps. Lessons Learned in implementing Sphere 2000–2002.* http://www.sphereproject.org/practice/less_learn.htm
2. http://www.projetqualite.org/fr/index/index.php
3. http://www.globalstudyparticipation.org/
4. See *Certification and Labelisation: a Blessing or a Curse? Proceeding of the 4 Autumn School on Humanitarian Affairs*, Groupe URD, Sept. 2005, http://www.urd.org/
5. Hugues Maury, 'What Is Evaluation For? The missing links in the evolution of the humanitarian actors, Humanitarian on the Move', Issue N°2; April 2009, http://www.urd.org/
6. Debating accountability, François Grünewald, Claire Pirotte and Véronique de Geoffroy in *Humanitarian Exchange*, Humanitarian Practice Network, no. 19, Sept. 2001, ODI. http://www.urd.org/fr/activites/publication/fichier/publispe_debatting_accountability.pdf
7. Paper presented at the FAO conference 'Food insecurity and disasters', Tivoli, 21–24 Sept. 2003.
8. Complexity and Context as the Determinants of the Future, Peter Walker, July 2008, https://wikis.uit.tufts.edu/confluence/display/FIC/Complexity+and+Context+as+the+Determinants+of+the+Future
9. http://www.compasqualite.org/en/dynamic-compas/index-dynamic-compas.php
10. http://www.coordinationsud.org/

6. LEARNING, MONITORING AND EVALUATION

1. L. Gosling and M. Edwards, *Toolkits: A Practical Guide to Assessment, Monitoring, Review, & Evaluation*, SCF UK, 1999.
2. B. Van de Putte, *Follow Up To Evaluations Of Humanitarian Programme*, ALNAP, 2001.
3. M. Patton, *Utilization-Focussed Evaluation: The New Century Text.* Thousand Oaks: Sage, 2008.
4. Alnap 2003: draft practitioner's handbook and global study monographs. See www.hapinternational.org for HAP publications: only HAP publications since 2005 are available here.
5. M. Edwards and D. Hulme, *NGOs Performance & Accountability: Beyond the Magic Bullet*, 1995.

6. Alnap 2003: draft practitioner's handbook and global study monographs. See www.hapinternational.org for hap publications.
7. Ibid.

7. INTERNATIONAL NGOS UNDER FIRE: CAUGHT BETWEEN THE GLOBAL FIGHT AGAINST TERRORISM AND NEO-LIBERAL APPROACHES TO SECURITY GOVERNANCE

1. Abby Stoddard, Adele Harmer and Victoria Di Domenico, *Providing Aid in Insecure Environments: 2009 Update, Trends in Violence Against Aid Workers and the Operational Response*, Humanitarian Policy Group (HPG) Policy Brief 34, Apr. 2009.
2. Andrea Binder and Jan Martin Witte, *Business Engagement in Humanitarian Relief: Key Trends and Policy Implications*, HPG Background Paper, ODI, London, Jun. 2007, pp. 3–4.
3. See Sami Makki, 'Privatisation de la sécurité et transformations de la guerre', *Politique étrangère*, n°4, IFRI (Paris), Winter 2004/2005.
4. In a study jointly financed by CARE and the UN Department of Humanitarian Affairs and conducted in 1999 as part of the Conflict Management Programme of Toronto University, the increased use of private security firms was recommended, due to the degradation in security conditions for humanitarian staff.
5. See Sami Makki, 'The Politicisation of Humanitarian Action and Staff Security: The Use of Private Security Companies by Humanitarian Agencies', Workshop Report, International Alert, London, Oct. 2001
6. For a deeper analysis of this problem see Abby Stoddard, Adele Harmer and Victoria DiDomenico, *The use of private security providers and services in humanitarian operations*, HPG Report 27, ODI, London, Oct. 2008.
7. US DoD, *Interagency Coordination During joint Operations Vol. 1*, Joint Publication 3–08, Washington, D.C., Department of Defense, 1996, p.v
8. Robert M. Cassidy, *Peacekeeping in the Abyss: British and American Doctrine and Practice after the Cold War*, Westport and London: Praeger, 2004, pp. 232–233.
9. Robert Egnell, *Complex Peace operations and Civil-Military Relations: Winning the Peace*, Routledge, 2009, p. 153.
10. InterAction, 'U.S. NGOs Welcome New White House Vision for Development', Press Release. http:// www.interaction.org/article/us-ngos-welcomes-new-white-house-vision-development (accessed online on 31/08/2010) and 'U.S. International Development and Humanitarian Organizations Should Have Stronger Role in Policymaking', InterAction Viewpoint, 17 Mar., 2009 (accessed online on 31 Aug. 2010).
11. See United States Institute of Peace, InterAction, Department of Defense, Guidelines for Relations Between US Armed Forces and Non-Governmen-

tal Humanitarian Organizations in Hostile or Potentially Hostile Environments, Washington, D.C., 2006.

12. According to Egnell, 'the CCO is designed to link civilian and military educators, trainers, thought leaders and practitioners to focus on the theoretical and practical problems associated with stability operations, counterinsurgency, and irregular warfare [and] to reach out to America's international partners and other allies to further civil-military operational response' with a civilian-military oversight and leadership (DoS, DoD and USAID). Egnell, Op.cit. p. 80

13. See Hans Binnendijk and Patrick Cronin (eds), *Civilian Surge: Key to Complex Operations*, Washington, D.C.: NDU Press, 2008.

14. Cassidy, Op.cit., pp. 228–9

15. Allied Administrative Publication 1 (AA1) in Michael Codner, *Hanging Together: Military Interoperability in an Era of Technological Innovation*, Whitehall Paper 56, Royal United Services Institute for Defence Studies, London, 2003, pp. 5–6.

16. See Security & Defence Agenda, Konrad Adenauer Stiftung, *NATO, the Credit Crunch and the New Security Environment*, a 17 Dec., 2009 International Conference Report, Brussels, 2010.

17. Egnell, *op.cit.*, pp. 153–5 and pp. 174–5.

18. EMA, *Concept et doctrine Interarmées de la coopération civilo-militaire*, PIA 09.100, Document n°262/DEF/EMA/EMP.1/NP, Paris: Ministère de la défense, Mar. 2005

19. Friis Arne Petersen, Hans Binnendijk, Charles Barry, and Peter Lehmann Nielsen, 'Implementing NATO's Comprehensive Approach to Complex operations' in Gülnur Aybet and Rebecca R. Moore (eds), *NATO in search of a Vision*, Washington, D.C.: Georgetown University Press, 2010, pp. 75–76.

20. ECHO: European Community Humanitarian Aid Office

21. Adele Harmer, 'Integrated Missions: A Threat to Humanitarian Security?', *International Peacekeeping*,Vol. 15 n°4, 2008, pp. 528—39.

8. PATRONAGE OR INFLUENCE?: INTERNATIONAL POLITICS AND THE CHANGING ROLE OF NON-GOVERNMENTAL HUMANITARIAN ORGANISATIONS

1. Abby Stoddard, 'Humanitarian NGOs: challenges and trends', in Joanna Macrae and Adele Harmer (eds), *Humanitarian Action and the Global War on Terror: A Review of Trends and Issues*, London: Overseas Development Institute, 2003.

2. Ibid.

3. InterAction, Speech given by Andrew Natsios, Administrator of USAID, at InterAction Conference, Washington, 21 May 2003.

4. Stoddard, 2003.

5. L. Minear and I. Smillie, *The Quality of Money: Donor behaviour in humanitarian financing*, Boston: Humanitarianism and War Project, The Feinstein International Famine Center, 2003.
6. M. Ignatieff, 'Empire Lite', Prospect 83, pp. 36–43
7. See for example N. de Torrente, 'Humanitarian action under attack: reflections on the Iraq War', *Harvard Human Rights Journal 1*, 2004. On HeinOnline.
8. J-H. Bradol, Introduction to F. Weissman (ed.), *In the Shadow of 'Just' Wars: Violence, Politics and Humanitarian Action*. Ithaca, New York: Cornell University Press, 2004.
9. D. Rieff, *A bed for the night: humanitarianism in crisis*. New York: Simon and Schuster, 2002.
10. A. Dewey, quoted in Carol Lancaster and Susan Martin 'The changing role of US aid policy in protracted crises', in J. Macrae, and A. Harmer (eds). *Beyond the Continuum: the changing role of aid policy in protracted crises*. HPG Report No 18, July 2004. London: ODI.
11. M. Ignatieff, 'Empire Lite', *Prospect* 83, 2003, pp. 36–43.
12. C. Messiant, *Why did Bicesse and Lusaka fail? A critical analysis*, Conciliation Resources, 2004, http://www.c-r.org/our-work/accord/angola/bicesse-lusaka.php#top.
13. Harmer and Macrae (eds), *Beyond the continuum: the changing role of aid policy in protracted crises*, HPG Report 18. London: ODI, 2004.
14. Rieff, 2002.
15. M. Duffield, J. Macrae, & D. Curtis, Editorial: 'Politics and Humanitarian Aid'. *Disasters* Journal Vol. 25 (4), 2001, pp. 269–274.
16. Harmer and Macrae (eds), *Beyond the continuum: the changing role of aid policy in protracted crises*, HPG Report 18. London: ODI, 2004.
17. Ignatieff, 2003.
18. T. Blair, Speech delivered to Chicago Economics Club, 22 April 1999.
19. N.J. Wheeler, S*aving strangers: humanitarian intervention in international society*, Oxford: Oxford University Press, 2000.
20. M. Walzer, *Just and Unjust Wars*, New York: Basic Books, 1992.
21. L. Roberts, et al. 'Mortality before and after the 2003 invasion of Iraq: cluster sample survey', *The Lancet*, Volume 364, Issue 9448, 2004, pp. 1857–1864.
22. Sami Makki, *Militarisation de l'humanitaire, privatisation du militaire*, Paris: CIRPES, 2005.
23. Hugo Slim, 'With or Against? Humanitarian Agencies and Coalition Counter-Insurgency', *Refugee Survey Quarterly*, 2004, upf.edu.

9. CHRISTIAN NGOS ON THE INTERNATIONAL SCENE: WHAT ARE THEIR MOTIVES?

1. Populorum Progressio encyclical. French edition: Apostolat des éditions, Lyon 1967. Presentation by Jean Rodhain, President of Caritas Internationalis.

USEFUL WEBSITES

NGO co-ordination platforms
European NGO Confederation (CONCORD) www.concordeurope.org
British Overseas NGOs for Development (BOND) www.bond.org.uk
Coordination Solidarité Urgence Développement (Coord SUD) www.coordination.org

Selected NGOs

Action Contre la Faim www.acffr.org
Care France www.carefrance.org
Centre for Humanitarian Dialogue (CHD) www.hdcentre.org
Comité catholique contre la faim et pour le développement (CCFD) www.ccfd.asso.fr
Handicap International www.handicapinternational.org
Islamic Relief www.islamicrelief.com
Médecins du Monde www.medecinsdumonde.org
Médecins Sans Frontières France www.msf.fr
Oxfam International www.oxfam.org.uk
The Save the Children Alliance www.savethechildren.org

International or multilateral organisations

International Committee of the Red Cross www.cicr.org
European Commission Humanitarian Aid Office (ECHO) http://europa.eu.int/comm/echo/index_fr.htm
United Nations Office for the Coordination of Humanitarian Affairs (OCHA) http://ochaonline.un.org/ Nations unies

Research Institutes

Centre d'études et de recherches internationales (CERI) www.cerisciencespo.com
Overseas Development Institute (ODI) www.odi.org.uk
Urgence Réhabilitation Développement (URD) www.urd.org
Conflict and Health Programme London School of Hygiene and Tropical Medicine www.lshtm.ac.uk/hpu/conflict/en

INDEX